THE
HAPPINESS
SCHEME

Martin Hill

*"When you have exhausted all possibilities, remember this, **you haven't**"* – THOMAS A EDISON

First published in Great Britain in 2016 by Bait Creations Ltd
Copyright © Martin Hill 2016
The Happiness Scheme

Contact: martinhill@thehappinessscheme.com

Thank you to Steven Mallinson for the design of a very original cover.

All rights are reserved. No part of this publication may be reproduced, stored in a retrieval system or transmitted in any form or by any means, electronic, mechanical, photocopying, recording or otherwise, without prior permission of the copyright owner and the publisher.

About The Author

Over the last six years Martin Hill has been the managing director of his own company. He has created and sold in excess of 1.5 million unique products to national and multi-national High Street chains in the UK.

His diverse career path has included labouring on a pig farm, driving cranes, selling communication solutions in an IT company and managing national accounts at a major PLC (to name just a few).

His grounding fundamental belief is that 'you have the power to change things' and that with hard work and intelligent application, you can succeed in almost any job or role you desire. Ultimately though, he believes the number one goal in life should be happiness, and assuring, no matter how allusive, anyone can find real happiness.

Martin has taken time out to pass on the techniques that he's found helpful. To strengthen his message, he's coupled these with current scientific research.

Even in the toughest of times, feeling hopeless should never be an option. There is always a window and always a door, you just have to keep looking.

"IF YOU'VE NEVER SEEN A DARK NIGHT,
YOU'VE NEVER SEEN THE STARS."

Disclaimer- The information in this book is for general guidance, and in no way whatsoever offers a substitute (or may be relied upon) for medical or professional guidance. Practice, regulations and research all change, please receive professional advice if you are in any doubt. The author and the publisher disclaim any liability arising directly or indirectly from the use, or misuse, of the information within the book or on the corresponding website.

Introduction

We all want happiness. It's now widely accepted that an attitude based on optimism and positivity leads to a longer and healthier life. The idea behind The Happiness Scheme is to give you the tools to create happiness and hold on to it. Likewise, a pessimistic mindset has been shown to cause stress, which can lead to a challenged immune system and potential health problems.

The Happiness Scheme is a response, an action plan, a way of fighting back the negativity. It's a plot to dispel the grey skies when they inevitably come. Just one happiness task can create a happiness cascade, raising your confidence and morale. One boost leads you to another, and suddenly you are creating a wheel of happiness that keeps on turning. Yes, there are still bumps, but this book aims to offer the right tools to cope.

I believe the skills within this book should be taught in schools, and I believe one day they will. The true measure of your life should not be how much material wealth you have accumulated, or how beautiful or handsome you are, but the amount of joy, peace, happiness and contentment you have.

Please feel free to jump straight to Part 3 of the book and start engaging in the activities in the 'Enjoying Life' section. If you're really short on time skip to Part 4 for 50 Quick Mood lifting tips and ideas.

Happiness is one of the noblest things to strive for. It benefits ourselves, our families, our friends, our work colleagues and even the random strangers we meet. Some research suggests [15] circumstances represent only ten percent of our happiness, in light of this fact this book hopes to demonstrate that...

'Happiness is a direct product of the goals you set, the thoughts and habits you hold, and your purposefully chosen attitude to life's events.'

"To affect the quality of the day, that is the highest of arts"

HENRY DAVID THOREAU

CONTENTS

PART 1: YOUR THOUGHTS

You were born for a reason	10
Who's in charge of what you think?	13
Productive and non-productive thinking	17
List your thoughts	20
Planting the new seeds and erasing the old	25
Master the brain	28
Positive thinking extends your life	31
Affirmations, your best self, confidence and the power stance	37

PART 2: LESSONS LEARNT

Karma	44
Let it go, let it go, let it go	47
The wonderful anti-stress button	50
Has the black dog come barking?	54
Mistakes	59
The 80/20 rule	61
There are only two ways to deal with a problem	65
Facing your fears	66
Experiencing the bad leads to the good	71
Problems, blame adversity and challenges	73
The news, social media and TV	77

CONTENTS

Maslow's hierarchy of needs — 80
Containing worry — 82
Don't overthink, be happy — 90

PART 3: ENJOYING LIFE

Gratitude — 94
Kindness — 96
Get off your bottom — 99
Excuses for stopping progress — 101
Get busy and create some new goals — 105
Your dreams are your best plan — 109
Change — 112
Just three good things per day — 115
Natural happiness hormones — 117
Now I can see you — 119
Seek out laughter — 121
I want to be the best — 123
Smile yourself happy — 125
Catching the flow — 127
Savour the moment — 130

PART 4: 50 QUICK MOOD LIFTERS

Quick Mood lifters — 133

PART 5: THE 5 MINUTE FOCUS — 150

PART 1: YOUR THOUGHTS

YOU WERE BORN FOR A REASON

"The best way to predict the future is to create it."
PETER DRUCKER

You were born for a reason: fact. It doesn't matter what's happened in the past or may happen in the future, you were born for a reason and successfully fulfilling your destiny is why you were born. It would be great if we had a plan given to us, a map to indicate how our life should be. However, there is a reason we don't get this delivered from some almighty dictator in the sky, the route and the choice must be chosen by you.

You are the sole driver and orchestrator of your life. Not your family or friends. You don't have to be anybody else's vision of perfect, only your own. Every individual has their own challenges, gene pool, and unique experiences. Yet we also have a tremendous ability to make things happen, the wonderful ability to make a change. Please fight away with every tendon in your body, and every individual neuron in your brain the thought that you may be inferior to anyone else. We all make mistakes, but allowing these to suppress our joy and capacity for good in the future is a waste of time. Tomorrow is far more important than yesterday.

You are going to need a touch of something that I wish you could bottle. It's a magical ingredient called confidence. It's amazing what just one gram of this stuff can do. You only need the smallest amount to make dramatic changes.

All the people I have met who have lived successful and happy lives have all been able to change something that wasn't working. This fundamental power to make changes comes from confidence.

Making something happen is what drives your life. Given that you are the managing director of your life, finding a gram of confidence is like finding a magic bean.

So here are three simple basic reasons (or if you like, three beans) to build a foundation of confidence.

Magic Bean 1 - *You're here NOW!*

You are here you are meant to be here. Congratulations, you've been chosen to live on the wonderful planet earth with all its natural beauty (including you). If you hadn't, you may have been living with aliens in some far-flung planet on the other side of the universe. So it's established, some celestial and almighty plan involved you being here, just like the Amazon rainforest and the Himalayan Mountains.

Magic Bean 2 - *You have a history of succeeding.*

Remember when you took your first steps as a child? You didn't know whether you could make those first few steps but you went for it. I'm guessing that after the first few steps you fell. Did that stop you trying again? No. You have a history of not being beaten.

Magic Bean 3 - *You've survived*

Whatever life has thrown at you, you've survived. Good time or bad, either way, you've made it through. So we were looking for a bean of confidence and now we have three. Pat yourself on the back, you've got what's required to start the journey to happiness.

Well done ...

YOU
HAVE A HISTORY OF SUCCESS AND
SURVIVAL

WHO'S IN CHARGE OF WHAT YOU THINK?

"It's only your opinion that matters"

It's quite amazing how much we store in our minds: memories of past events and consequential worries of potential future outcomes. Let's think about these worries for a moment:

1. Our appearance
2. What others think about us and our actions
3. How popular we are
4. How well or badly we will do something

We all like praise, but it's the negative stuff that we allow through that we need to contain. This negativity can create dangerous blocks for us, if we let it.

So who have we listened to, to allow these concerns? Well remarkably there are many outside influences:

- Your mum, dad, grandparents or guardians
- Your partner
- Your teachers

- Your friends
- Your enemies
- Your brothers and sisters
- Your boss
- You

So it can be rather complex juggling these influences to come to a rational perception of yourself. That is, until you realise two very important facts:

FACT 1 – It's only your opinion that matters

Please read the following poem adapted from Dale Wimbrow:
When you get what you want in your struggle for gain and the world makes you King or Queen for the day.
Just go to the mirror look at yourself and see what that person has to say.
For it isn't your mother or father or friend whose judgment you must pass.
The one whose opinion matters most in your life is the one looking back from the glass.
For this is the one you must satisfy, for they are with you right up till the end.
And you will have passed your most difficult test when the one in the glass is your friend.
Now you may be the one who gets a good break and think you're a wonderful guy.
But the one in the glass says you're only a fake if you can't look them straight in the eye.

FACT 2 - You have the freedom to choose how to respond to events

Please see the following from Viktor Frankl (a psychiatrist) who was imprisoned for five years in a Nazi concentration Camp. He states (abridged)

"Everything in life can be taken from you except one thing... your freedom to choose HOW you will respond to a situation. This is what determines the quality of the life we've lived. Not rich or poor, healthy or unhealthy ...what determines our quality of life is how we respond to events and what state of mind we allow them to trigger"

IT'S ALL ABOUT YOU (1)

Fact 1 affirms that it is no one else's opinion or influence that matter. Not your friends, family or work colleagues. Obviously it's courteous to listen, as they may have your best interests at heart, but ultimately it's your life and you must follow your heart and dreams.

In Fact 2 our friend Victor tells us "what determines our quality of life is how we respond to events and what state of mind we allow them to trigger".

So now we just need to put ourselves on the right path and after some consideration I'm sure you will realise that eventually, irrespective of how we cut it...

HAPPINESS IS A CHOICE

Some suggest that there may be a genetic link to our happiness. This is addressed by the University of Minnesota's Professor Emeritus of Psychology David Lykken, PhD. He said:

"Happiness is genetically influenced but NOT genetically fixed.

*The brain's structure **CAN** be modified through practice. If you really want to be happier than your grandparents provided for in your genes, you have to learn the kinds of things you can do, day by day, to bounce your set point up and avoid the things that bounce it down"*

This is exceptionally reassuring news. We can, in effect, mould ourselves happy. We can take the clay we are given and manipulate, shape and form it into something better by adopting good attitudes and behaviours.

HAPPINESS REALLY IS A CHOICE

Of course you could sit on your butt all day drifting through life, doing nothing, and thinking anything that popped into your head. Well I 100% agree with Disraeli, a former English Prime Minister when he said,

'there is no happiness without action'.

The goals you set, the thoughts you think, and your purposely chosen attitude to life's events dictate your happiness. So it's time to start working on the most important person in the world:

YOU!

PRODUCTIVE AND NON-PRODUCTIVE THINKING

"Change your thoughts and your thoughts change your world" NORMAN VINCENT PEALE

After leaving school, I did a lot of manual labour to earn some money. To be honest the money was good and I managed to save a lot, but I found the job depressing. This was the first time I had been really challenged. I went to the local bookstore to see if I could find something to change my mood and uplift me. To this day I am grateful for finding Norman Vincent Peale's book 'The Power of Positive Thinking'.

Dr Peale suggested that an inflow of new thoughts could alter your perception of events; that thoughts possessed a forceful power. He thought that we could think ourselves into situations and also out of situations. If we thought in one particular way we would receive that set of circumstances and if we thought in another way would get an entirely different set of circumstances.

This book 'blew my mind' and really uplifted me. If the author's suggestions were true, then it wasn't the depressing job that mattered, it was my approach to it. So... cutting lumps of cold steel repeatedly on a noisy machine, starting at 7:30 in the morning and working outside in the depths of winter wasn't my idea of a dream job. But, if I could stick it out a little longer by changing how I thought about it (today this is known as re-framing), I could begin my search for something else.

I decided to put a smile on my face (little did I realise at the time how beneficial this was), accept my situation, work hard and find something else that fulfilled me more down the line. I was eventually promoted to crane driver and then went to work on a pig farm. This was just the beginning of what turned into a variety of different and interesting jobs.

Just because things may not be ideal for you now, that does not mean things won't be in the future. Be confident and believe in yourself. The present is just one chapter. Trust me, there are many more chapters to come. You can find a new path, you can find the right door, and you **CAN** find the silver lining of the cloud. You can grow stronger and more resourceful, all it takes is the courage to keep going. With practice, you can make a habit of thinking productively for the rest of your life.

All computers, phones and technologies run from scientific principles born in research laboratories. They automatically follow the guidelines they are programmed to. Your brain is exactly the same: it obeys the instructions you give to it. The good news is we can form new neural networks and change the way we view things.

Conscious decisions are often taken from us by the habits and patterns we've developed ourselves, which can be both good and bad. I like to call these cow tracks. If you've ever watched cows in a field (I was once a farm worker), you'll know that they always take the same habitual path to the water trough. They could be 50 yards from the water trough, but they will travel 200 yards to get there. They have programmed themselves to go down a regular path and they will not attempt another route.

Fortunately, we are substantially more intelligent than cows and can make better decisions and adjust our habits. To start with we need to develop more of the good habitual thinking habits and let go of the bad. I like to call this productive and non-productive thinking and it is my belief that

> **Productive (good/positive) thinking contributes to happiness**
>
> **AND**
>
> **Non-productive (bad/negative) thinking contributes to sadness**

To train your brain to think productively, you will need to be disciplined and willing to break old habits (bad cow tracks). Throughout our lives, we will inevitably experience many events that we perceive as both good and bad, but actually these are just viewpoints. How we deal with these or categorise them is completely down to the choices we make.

One of the toughest things I've experienced is losing someone I loved. We are human and not unfeeling and will obviously need sufficient time to adjust to loss, but I have found immense comfort in the celebration of having had something special.

Please see two great quotes from Dr. Seuss (Theodor Seuss Geisel) a celebrated American writer.

> *"Don't cry because it's over. Smile because it happened"*

> *"You have brains in your head. You have feet in your shoes. You can steer yourself any direction you choose."*

Events can sometimes happen that we have absolutely no control over. These events may be exceptionally challenging, but how you respond to these events is in your control.

> *"You cannot control the wind, or where it comes from, but you can control the sails"*

LIST YOUR THOUGHTS

"When you stop chasing the wrong things, you give the right things a chance to catch you." - LOLLY DASKAL

The only way we can affect anything is to first of all assess a situation, or measure it. This is the fundamental basis of mechanics and science and is the idea behind this chapter. It is also very liberating getting your thoughts down on paper rather than in your head. It gives you a visual reference to study to make better decisions.

Self-talk is classified by the Mayo Clinic as "the endless stream of unspoken thoughts that run through your head... that can be positive or negative." When you are challenged by specific situations, or want to come to terms with something, it should be helpful to compile your thoughts.

When you feel the need grab a pen and paper (or the notes section on your tablet, phone etc.) and start detailing your thoughts.

Once you have compiled them you can begin to double-check their authenticity. Go through each thought and ask yourself this simple question.

"Is this a productive or non-productive thought?"

Mixed within the justifications of your thoughts will be a selection of both positive and negative thinking. Both of these play very important roles, but we need to be careful to not let the potential negative and non-productive thoughts trump the positive way forward.

I can actually see a case for negative thinking but this is a little complex so let's cover this now. To evaluate a situation correctly, you need to look at potential pitfalls too. If you're not careful though these 'potential' negative outcomes can stunt and blind you to the point where you don't take the first step to make something really positive happen. I have wrestled with this experience in my personal life and business but now have a good strategy to cope with it.

Non-productive thoughts can really be powerful so watch out for them, these should NEVER conquer our march forward, so I like to:

1) Consider them
2) Make a careful plan for dealing with them
3) Mentally parcel them up and put them on the bottom shelf and completely forget them while I focus and believe 100% on the desired 'good' outcome.

I like the analogy of walking through a minefield. If you know the mines are there it would be madness to run through it. But if you had the right piece of kit to remove every single mine, you could run through happily enjoying the sunshine with no problems.

'So deal with the mines, so you can enjoy the run'

After you've made your plans, and covered every angle, if your negative thoughts return, write them down and

THROW THEM IN THE BIN!

There is good research showing how productive this simple act is (2). Why is it so important to dismiss any negative and unproductive thoughts? This is best summed up in the next powerful statement.

The statement comes from psychological scientists Maryanne Garry and Robert Michael of Victoria University of Wellington, along with Irving Kirsch of Harvard Medical School and Plymouth University. They delve into the phenomenon of suggestion, exploring the intriguing relationship between suggestion, cognition, and behaviour. The article was published in an issue of Current Directions in Psychological Science:

'Once we anticipate a specific outcome will occur, our subsequent thoughts and behaviours will actually help to bring that outcome to fruition."
I will break this down:

Part 1 *"Once we anticipate a specific outcome will occur"*

If you are envisaging that you can't have a happier life, you probably won't. This is also known as the power of suggestion. The power behind suggestions is phenomenal, and the wonderful thing is you are the writer and author of your own suggestions. YOU are the captain of the ship. You write the future, no one else. The power of positive suggestions can improve people's lives. If you can accept this, then it is time to start anticipating and embracing some good outcomes for yourself.

Part 2 *"our subsequent thoughts and behaviours will actually help to bring that outcome to fruition".*

What explains these effects? The answer lies in our 'response expectancies,' or the ways in which we anticipate our responses in various situations. These expectancies set us up for automatic responses that actively influence how we get to the outcome we expect. So more simply put a thought is purely a prediction of what may occur.

Whether that thought sinks or swims is completely down to us. It is our conscious choice.

So if you don't like a particular thought,

1) Mentally 'extinguish it' like you would a candle
2) Dream one up that is more pleasing to you to replace it.

Be creative with your mental imagery, visualise and 'fully believe' your desired outcome. Eventually and with practice, new neural pathways will be created and you will literally rewire your brain and create a whole new mindset.

So let's go back to your list. Anything on your list under 'productive thoughts' must suggest a positive outcome in the future. Remember you must always predict positive, good, productive outcomes because:

"Our subsequent thoughts and behaviours will actually help to bring that outcome to fruition".

In a simple example, famous English footballer Michael Owen once said (after scoring a fabulous winning goal in a match)

"I just expected to do it"

If you don't think your going to do something then you're never going to do it until you dream or believe that you can. You used to dream as a kid, so please get some good dreaming in now.

Ultimately, people largely get what they expect in life, so let's begin expecting some really good things. Start imagining those suggested optimistic outcomes. They are phenomenally powerful and they can dramatically change your life for the better.

Albert Einstein recognised this and in 1929 said....

"Imagination is more important than knowledge. Knowledge is limited. Imagination encircles the world."

I believe the above to be a truly amazing quotation from one of the most eminent scholars to walk the earth.

PLANTING THE NEW SEEDS AND ERASING THE OLD

"In the heart of adversity lies a greater potential benefit"

Now you have completed your thought list, you will hopefully see the benefits of the productive thoughts and how they can benefit you. Yes, an inflow of new positive, optimistic and productive thoughts can remake you.

So now is the time to edit your list, anything in the 'productive thoughts' column is absolutely fine, just leave it there. These thoughts give you confidence.

Now let's attend to the non-productive thoughts. If these are largely consisting of worries, see the further chapter on containing worry. In a quick summary though, worries come from potential problems. The more you focus on something the more you will see. I have deliberated for days over business issues to finally come up with a simple solution that was staring me in the face all the time.

Sometimes we focus too much on the issue or problem and not enough on the solution. Moving your focus to a solution is key to reducing worry. Again getting things out of your head and writing things down will help you gain a better perspective. After you've worked exceptionally hard, given it your best shot and done everything you possibly can to creatively address the problem, what more can you do?

Well here are a few questions you can ask yourself about your unproductive thoughts, mines or bad cow tracks:

1) How can I view this differently, is there another perspective that I am missing?
There are thousands of ways to view things. Find a viewpoint that allows you to move on. Then mentally stick these thoughts on the bottom shelf and move on.

2) Have I looked at this thoroughly, given it as much attention as possible and done everything I possibly can?
If the answer is 'yes', then stop worrying about it. You can do no more. Stick these thoughts on the bottom shelf and move on.

3) Have I come up against this sort of thing before and how did I handle it then?
Look back, how have you dealt with similar situations in the past? Once you've worked through this, stick these thoughts on the bottom shelf and move on.

4) Could this event drive me in a new direction?
'In the heart of adversity lies a greater potential benefit'. This could create a whole new magnificent and wonderfully interesting path. Once you have your new path, stick the worrisome thoughts on the bottom shelf and move on.

I'm sure you've picked up the 'move on' bit now. We can only do what we can do so let's mentally parcel things up and stick them on the bottom shelf when we know we can do no more.

Perhaps it is time to change direction and move into other more fulfilling areas or maybe you can come to terms with your new situation even though it may not be where you thought you would land. It might be that you need to reframe or change the way you think about something.

Ultimately, any non-productive thoughts need to be erased from your life. They are time wasters, joy killers, and useless to you and your future happiness. Remember the cow tracks? That's exactly what these thoughts are. If you'd like some more happiness in your life, erasing these old tracks or at least not travelling down them is going to help considerably. You're creating a new world now... leave the old one behind.

So start a new uplifting list to replace your old unproductive thoughts and add to it regularly. Seek out new optimistic thoughts, "I'm great at learning new things" and "I love walks in the countryside" for example.

Chris Williams Professor of Psychosocial Psychiatry at the University of Glasgow suggests having at least five things on your list and adding to it regularly. Keep your list in a place where you see it routinely (the fridge door, the note section on your phone) to remind yourself of your new beliefs.

If your negative or non-productive thoughts return treat them as imposters and dismiss them. Let's try a few suggestions in the next chapters to create a shift and take your thoughts into a new direction.

MASTER THE BRAIN

"It is as if the whole universe changes when we look at it"

As mentioned earlier our brain is sending us messages all day, we just need to make sure it is telling us the right things. By learning new ways of doing things and deciding to adapt your mental behaviour you are making a new choice and determining where you are going. I am a huge believer in taking as little as a two-minute focused breathing pause when under a lot of pressure (please also see the chapter The wonderful anti-stress button).

The more often you pause the more often you get chance to obtain some clarity to your thoughts and emotions.

When your emotions are running away and your thoughts are unconscious rather than conscious your intentions can get lost. My grandparents used to say, when you're stressed count to 10... good advice Gran! This gives you chance to think about things and come up with a better more considered decision. You give yourself the opportunity to interrupt any non-productive self-chatter and get back on track.

If we accept the fact that we get 'more of what we focus on' we can choose how we relate our thoughts by focusing on mental paths that are beneficial to us, and not going down roads that are bad for us. Repetition drives the opportunity for our thoughts and actions to be manifested.

This is how habits are created. Actively look at your mental habits: are they serving you well or working against you?

In her book 'Awakening the Brain' Charlotte A. Tomaino PhD and clinical neuropsychologist states:

"When you are aware of how a choice you make will impact your brain in the future, you are awake to influencing your own development"

If you search for anything on Google it will produce the results you ask for. Your brain is the just same, it searches for things to substantiate your thoughts. In effect you get more of what you are looking for.

Lets go off track a little. In the study of the very small pieces of our universe 'Quantum Mechanics' there is a very significant test called the Double Slit Experiment, which involves studying particles or atoms of light. This experiment was first carried out over 200 years ago, and whist its properties are well understood, the fundamental causes for the behaviour of the particles is a complete mystery to this day. Crucially, and in a presently unexplained manner, the particles change their behaviour when observed...WHAT!!

It is as if the whole universe changes when we look at it.

Please authenticate this for yourself on YouTube by searching for the Double Slit Experiment. I like to take these findings as evidence that things change depending on how we view them. Now science categorically supports this.

Don't let your views, thoughts and emotions take charge of you. YOU can control them:

1. Pause (take a walk if necessary)

2. Take stock of the situation from a relaxed standpoint, if required do something to distract yourself and then come back to it.
3. Return and make good new neural networks (mental cow tracks), foreseeing good optimistic outcomes and suggestions to improve the situation, then use your creativity to:

Multiply them in every way possible!

WILL POSITIVE THINKING EXTEND YOUR LIFE?

"My interest is in the future because I am going to spend the rest of my life there" CHARLES KETTERING

It is exceptionally helpful to frame events well in order to foster positive thinking. For instance I follow my local football team and have noticed that when we are losing 1-0 with 3 minutes left on the clock I am disappointed, because I think we are going to lose. Yet when we score a goal in the last minute and draw 1-1 it feels like a win and I go home feeling like we've won. We haven't won, we've only got 1 point where a win would get us 3 points, but it 'feels so much more' than just a point and I go home happy.

When I have a night out with friends I'm always conscious of one particular good friend who takes great pride in his appearance. His hair is perfectly groomed and his clothes never have even one minor crease in them. We give him lots of stick, but in fairness he always looks quite good. However, on a couple of occasions, someone else has walked into the pub with an identical shirt on. My friend's fashion consciousness has now taken one big dive, which in honesty we find very amusing (in a friendly way).

His shirt is still the same great shirt it was when he walked in, but now there are two in the room and it's lost a lot of its coolness. On this occasion the framing has been changed for our amusement.

Relationships sometimes run their course, too. We can beat ourselves up and lament for a while or celebrate the fact that they happened, look for new horizons and move on. Equally we could say "your loss, my gain" and/or secretly call your ex an idiot for splitting up with you. The idea behind all this is to frame your thinking so it ultimately leaves you in a good place.

Things are not what they are, they are what we THINK they are or perceive them to be. It depends how we frame them. Don't beat yourself up with comparisons, these are ridiculous. Sometimes it's a question of 3 steps forward 2 steps back. The main thing is to never ever give up. To affirm a quote attributed to George A. Custer

"It's not how many times you get knocked down that count, it's how many times you get back up"

Framing yourself events or things badly is completely unproductive and is not going to assist you at all. It helps to be passionately creative here, so take some real time out to search for a positive frame on events.

Some psychologists may refer to this as Cognitive Therapy. There are practitioners of this profession available, the principal of which is studying your thoughts to eradicate incorrect or unhelpful thoughts, emotions and behaviours. Once this is complete, the therapist then guides you along thoughts and behaviours that are going to help you thrive, rather than dive. Of course this is perfectly possible to do with some real creativity yourself.

Struggling to find other possible ways of viewing things? Let's go look at our trusted friend science for a moment. Some very eminent mathematicians and cosmologists now predict the possibility of a potential multiverse that is full of 'infinite possibilities'.

What happens if I turn left, what happens if I turn right?

On each occasion anything different could happen and the results could be completely different. The ideas in this arena have now moved from fantasy and science fiction into mainstream science. There are always an INFINITE number of paths you could tread, each one with a completely different outcome.

Every time before you flip a coin to make a 'minor decision' there are two potential possibilities, however, once it's flipped, we only experience one of them (obviously this shouldn't be done for major decisions that need correct and focused attention).

Every time the coin is flipped the universe effectively splits into two separate worlds of possibility. In science these multiple possibilities, which exist everywhere, are known as the 'Hilbert Space'. Quantum computing is now using the quantum world of multiple 'potential possibilities' to develop superfast computers.

So, as science definitively shows us, things can be viewed in literally 'trillions' of different ways and from many different perspectives. Beating yourself up and being hard on yourself is never productive. There are many other outcomes and possibilities; you just need to look for them. So please take some real creative time out to 'positively frame' events so that you can move forward in the best possible w a y .

"View yourself in the best possible light"

Research has shown that positive people live quite substantially longer (on average), so bearing this in mind, it's very well worthwhile cultivating a positive mind-set.[3] Yes there are going to be a few storms in everyone's life and we never know when they are going to come, but maintaining a positive outlook and believing that things will improve will help you considerably.

Be careful what you tell yourself, because you may be telling yourself the wrong things daily.

It may take some time to develop a positive mind-set, but the challenge of viewing things in a positive way has now been shown to extend your life. We can make ourselves miserable or we can make ourselves strong, the amount of effort is just about the same.

One well-respected National Clinic reported that positive people live longer lives by almost 20 %! Why this should be is still a little unclear, but my guess is that positive people are probably getting a lot less stressed. Stress releases a hormone called Cortisol and it is currently suggested that too much Cortisol can have a negative effect on the immune system and also impede learning.

Whatever the link is finally proven to be, it is now accepted that mind and body are linked.

A positive mind-set may lead to a longer life.

Between 1962 and 1965 researchers from the Mayo Clinic interviewed over 1,100 patients, asking them about their view of life. They then tracked these people for the next thirty years to see if they could pick up any significant differences between members of the group.

They found that the most optimistic people had nearly a 20% better chance of still being alive. This is an incredible statistic and when flipped on its head means that the most pessimistic people regretfully met their grave earlier. This surely generates a call to action to think optimistically and positively on a 'day to day' basis.

Earlier chapters are full of techniques to help you on the way to positive and productive thinking; it really is just a question of you actively telling your mind to search for an optimistic outcome. With time, you will be amazed at how creative and alert you can become when always looking for positive outcomes.

It really is just a habit!

Have you ever heard of the saying 'fake it till you make it'. There is a remarkable truth here, but I prefer to view things with two simple words that I'd be delighted you took with you wherever you go they are...

'AS IF'

This concept is astounding. You mentally wear the clothes and facets of a state you desire, you simply behave 'AS IF' you already are that person. I have tried this successfully for many years and can personally vouch for its success. You can conjure up the person you want be at any time in your mind. Simply imagine that person is you and away you go. Wherever you go, whatever you do you simply behave 'AS IF' you are already in the state you desire. Maybe there are a number of states you like? I know a good friend that has repeated the following for decades and to be honest this is very much the person I see him as. He simply repeats these words whenever he wants to feel them within himself.

Joy, Enthusiasm, Brightness, Laughter and Love

So choose your own heartfelt, positive, well-meaning and upbeat words and states wisely, as repeating these words and the associated thoughts will assist greatly in bringing them to fruition within you.

Take control of your life! You're the boss... master your moods and quite simply behave **as if** you are the person you want to become and before too long that amazing person will emerge.

Write your own five words down on your preferred device, but keep it handy until you memorise them. Repeat them regularly through the day and refine them if you wish. Imagine yourself in this state and expressing the meaning behind the words. If you do this regularly with time and practise, you will grow into this person, expressing the very traits you desire.

Behave like a happy person and you will be... behave like a sad person you will be! It really is just a self-fulfilling prophecy.

Please try a quick positive thinking exercise. Sit down, relax and close your eyes. Concentrate on only your breathing for five minutes. If a thought comes, let it go and go back to your breathing. Your brain is comparable to a hard working muscle it needs resting too.

Clearing your thoughts will give more room for new thoughts to come forward. After five minutes start to create and imagine a bright NEW future for yourself in the fire of your imagination and thoughts. Paint pictures in your mind of positive outcomes. These really do have power. Trust me, they are in there.

Allow your subconscious to bring them forward. If it helps create a bubble chart or write some positive words down. Keep these in your notebook, phone, tablet or diary. It's helpful to have these with you so you can frequently refer to them to underline where you are going.

Think negatively, you will get negative results. Think positively, you will get positive results...

Remember this statement from an earlier chapter,

'Once we anticipate a specific outcome will occur, our subsequent thoughts and behaviours will actually help to bring that outcome to fruition'

This is the spark that lights the fire. This is where it happens. IMAGINING you can do it is the start. The world is a canvas to our imagination. Start dreaming again and make your life the way you want it to be! Fully believe:

"I CAN DO THIS"

After all, if you focus on the past that's all you're going to get more of. To borrow that famous quote from the film Star Wars...

'Your focus determines your reality'

One of the most important things to know is that irrespective of circumstances you have the power to change things!

AFFIRMATIONS, YOUR BEST SELF, CONFIDENCE AND THE POWER STANCE

"We are what we repeatedly do. Excellence then is not an act, but a habit." ARISTOTLE

As was mentioned in a previous chapter when I was a teenager I did jobs that I didn't particularly enjoy, but they paid reasonably well so I stuck with them. The great Norman Vincent Peale and his Power of Positive Thinking book kept me sane and this was my first experience of positive affirmations and expectations. He was one of the pioneers in this field and his Christian faith helped him put across new concepts of psychology.

We build up feelings of security or insecurity by how we think. The power of thought is exceptionally influential on our feelings and emotions. However, help is on the horizon in the form of positive self-affirmations (4). We just need to create some for ourselves. You may think this a little weird, but trust me you are currently affirming things to yourself every day. The difference is, these are in your head and not on a piece of paper or written in notes in your favourite electronic device.

What we are simply doing here is training your brain to go in the direction YOU have chosen it to go in, rather than let it go where it wants.

Think of a young puppy dog on a lead. It wants to go where it likes and pulls against its owner. With time though the young puppy obeys its master and happily walks alongside. This is what we are going to do with the mind, we're giving it a little discipline, to show it what direction we want it to go in rather than let it wander off. Once you've cracked this, it really is quite an incredible accomplishment and one that can reshape your whole life.

When reciting your new affirmations to yourself (out loud or in your mind) try combining these with some positive visualisations; pictures or mental images of you holding your desired state and how to get there. Whatever you can imagine or dream can significantly enhances the chances of it coming to reality so really believe you can do this.

It is vitally important not to light up the 'counter argument' in your mind when making your affirmations. Your mind isn't stupid. It knows what's going on. What we're doing is training or framing it to think in another way that it will accept; effectively creating another thought that is going to be beneficial to you and provide a basis for 'thriving instead of diving'. Remember this:

Repetition drives the opportunity for our thoughts and actions to be manifested 'FACT' so let's engage good thoughts.

So to a few examples to give you an idea of how it works. I don't know exactly what your end goals are, but here are a few common ones. These are here for guidance only, so please feel free to create your own affirmations.

Weight Loss - Now if you wanted to lose some weight you could repeat

"I want to lose my extra weight"

Let's look at this statement in more detail. This is confirming that you have the extra weight and that you want to, but aren't! Not a great statement to repeat to yourself at all. Look at the difference here.

"Today I'm eating the correct portions of a healthy diet of fruit, vegetables and a small amount of protein because I know this will help me lose weight"

At least this way you have more chance of success. It is a positive and clear statement.

Job Interview – It's equally important to avoid negative speech. So, if preparing for an interview, don't say:
 'Today I'm not going to get nervous'

You might say instead

"I've researched this thoroughly, I really know my areas of expertise, and so my success is guaranteed because I'm committed to preparation and hard work."

Take note of the statement 'my success is guaranteed'. You must go into battle with thoughts of victory! Anticipating that you will be a winner will enhance your chances of success significantly.

If you don't happen to succeed, bounce back, learn from it and get ready for the next step. Remember, life loves a trier.

A social situation – When you meet new people, try the following statement by the wonderful Tom Hopkins in his book The Official Guide to Success:

"It's amazing, but nearly everyone I meet really likes me right off. Of course, I like almost everyone I meet right away, too. I guess the way I feel about people shows"

You can write your own self-affirmations and put them in visible places. The important thing is to repeat them regularly to yourself through the day. I personally like having a system in place whereby I read my affirmations in the morning, noon and night. I recommend reading each one three times before moving to the next one. However, repeat and alter them as often as you wish.

Once you have your new thoughts in place, you may only need to repeat them during challenging times. I still refer to my old affirmations, as they are permanently and joyfully etched into my mind.

This exercise isn't intended to make you arrogant, but to fill you with confidence when you need it. Don't be afraid to praise yourself, it will bolster you in time of need.

So, to summarise your affirmations:

1) Decide and set your chosen goal and your plan of how to attain it. Feel free to adjust and change this at any time.
2) Don't write anything that is overwhelming or unattainable.
3) Say your goal out loud with real passion and energy. Most importantly, BELIEVE in your future goal.
4) Avoid negatives like "I will not", or "I cannot"."

This isn't an exam, so I urge you to try it. You will be amazed by its power. Please don't worry if your affirmation is not working the way you want it to, either. Tweak and adjust it until you find something that works for you.

The 'best possible self' scenario.

If you are not a particular fan of the daily affirmation technique, this comparable technique involves writing in your own journal or electronic device. You may have the same goals, but simply write about them whenever you wish. The key to this approach is to follow the plan above, considering positive visualisations of your 'best possible self'. Imagine yourself achieving your goals. Imagine the path you would take to get there. You have succeeded, you have conquered, and you have done it: you have turned your dreams into reality.

This technique does have some advantages as it enables you to regularly plan, change and direct your strategy to reach your goals. It is more time consuming but very effective. Use the technique, which best works for you. As we are all different you are more likely to carry out the tasks that resonate with you most, so keep it fresh and try different things until you find something that works for you.

This is your future. You should leave no stone unturned if you want to achieve your goals. Whatever you can imagine, or dream that you can achieve, will significantly enhance the chances of it becoming a reality.

A little more on confidence

Confidence is an important thing for all of us. We all want to succeed, but some of us can be weighed down with nerves. Trust me this is an excellent reflex to have. Nerves show that you care passionately! The same nerves you have now kept your ancestors alive in the jungle. We are tuned to imagine potential scenarios that could potentially hurt us, although just like our thoughts, these are often not true. You're simply highly geared for survival (the flight or fight response). However, it's helpful to control our nerves and thoughts in the same way that sports stars like footballers, tennis players and golfers do before big games.

Sports physiologists are masters of this but the same techniques apply to your daily life. You simply need to calm your mind. This is discussed in the chapter 'The Wonderful Anti-Stress Button', which discusses how to relax your mind through breathing exercises. This is now widely known as mindfulness.

Of course you may have an odd fall on your new path, but please keep believing in your new future self and

'HOLD ON'

Tripping up is a normal, it's perfectly acceptable, you may mark yourself three out of ten... that's fine! Just keep focusing on increasing your score. Remember to <u>create that picture</u> in your head of your **'very best self'** and **trust** that person will turn up.

The Power Stance

As strange as it may seem, some excellent studies by Amy Cuddy (PhD, MA, BA) have shown that if we stand tall, pull our shoulders back and thrust our arms out, we can raise our confidence levels substantially.

Try this when you are repeating your affirmations. In essence, your mind obeys your body.

Power stance example

Yes unbelievably there is real science behind this. If you have any doubts, check out the fearsome New Zealand All Blacks 'haka' (traditionally used by the Maori people) and see the effect it has on their motivation.

Part 2
LESSONS LEARNT

KARMA

"The best way to cheer yourself up is to try cheer somebody else up" MARK TWAIN

In eastern religions the concept of karma is widely believed. The principle is based on the fact that your actions influence your future. Good intentions and actions lead to happiness (good karma) and bad intentions and actions lead to unhappiness (bad karma). The simple statement is often used to emphasise this point

'what goes around comes around'.

There is a similar quotation in the Bible:

'For whatever one sows, that will he also reap'

This is a simple philosophy, which I believe in 99% of the time. The missing 1% is attributed to the fact that we cannot predict the future accurately. The future is open to events beyond our comprehension, both good and unfortunately bad. Karma is 'NOT' a perfect model. However, when negative things happen, it is how we respond to them that impacts our lives.

'Our ultimate destiny in life is programmed by how we respond to events and what state of mind we allow them to trigger'

You may sail through life without any bad luck at all. I sincerely hope you do. However, most of us will face challenges at some point in our lives. In my humble opinion, this may have nothing to do with karma. This is just how life on this planet is constructed. Perhaps we are challenged to help us grow into stronger and more capable people. In turn this strength gives us more empathy and understanding towards others.

Mindful of the 99% and 1%, it makes sense to engage with the 99% and deal with the 1% of bad luck if it happens. Why? Because going back to the research by the psychological scientists at Victoria University of Wellington, Harvard Medical School and Plymouth University.

'Once we anticipate a specific outcome will occur, our subsequent thoughts and behaviours will actually help to bring that outcome to fruition'

It's my belief that karma applies 99% of the time, so what can we do to initiate a bit of good karma? For me, this is best summarised by the multiple ways one can be kind.

'No drug in the world will make you feel more complete inside your inner soul than showing kindness to other people'.

Once we do a genuinely nice thing for someone else, we get a nice feeling inside. Not only that, the favour is normally returned, too. It creates a positive circle of good will that just keeps growing.

A smile works in the same way. If you smile at someone, they will generally smile in return, and that simple smile could lift their whole day. In much the same way, just one positive person in a room can affect the whole room at a party. Give someone a bit of your time, be a good listener, and you will be utterly staggered at what this can do for them and for you. Simply spreading a bit of love will fulfil you in ways you cannot imagine.

The other side of karma, is its darker side. If we wish others ill, these thoughts may manifest themselves back towards us. If we are selfish, people will no longer want to be with us. I have seen this happen on many occasions. Ultimately, if you feel wronged, don't worry: keep calm and allow karma to finish it.

LET IT GO... LET IT GO ... LET IT GO

"Don't lock yourself in a self-defeating jail"

Harbouring resentment towards others is a natural reaction when you have been mistreated. However, such feelings can eventually eat into you if not controlled. You may have been criticised or let down, but for the sake of your own health, try to move on and forgive.(5) If we hold on to grievances, we hold back happiness. It's like locking yourself in self-defeating jail. It really is your choice, your blockage, and you can let it go anytime.

A comment might even come from someone you love. We all get a bad day sometimes, and a touch of negative drift. This can come from simple things like being stuck in traffic, a bad day at the office, a bad thought, overhearing someone else's woes, the news on the television, a spot on your face. The list goes on. Don't be too hard on yourself if you sometimes behave negatively. We aren't angels, we're humans and we all make mistakes. Remember that before you judge yourself, or others too harshly.

Negative drift can affect us in two ways. First, if we're having a bad day it could make us short tempered or irritable. We may not even be aware of this sometimes, as we are so focused on the most important thing in our mind. The second way that negative drift affects us, is the way our perception of events becomes skewed. If we're having a bad day, or perhaps we're ill, our disposition and mood is seriously affected, leaving us open to viewing events negatively when they were never meant to be.

You may have conquered your thoughts and be in a nice place when out of the blue comes a comment from someone else that is either a direct criticism, or you view as a negative comment. Whichever it may be, other people have to struggle with their own insecurities. All you need to do is smile and laugh it off, and show them no ill feeling.

Whilst some people are on a completely different page to you there are others who are very similar. You can't be close friends with everyone (even though you might want to be). You can perceive people like the wavelengths of a radio, accept that you'll be tuned in to some just perfectly and others will be more distant.

It may be that in your life you have been fortunate enough to have been nurtured by the love of kind people while you were young (your guardians or parents). I believe this is a huge factor in making you feel secure in your adult years. Experiencing love in your early years is a stabilising influence on your later life. If you have been fortunate, try to forgive anyone who may not have been as fortunate as you. They may be troubled with insecurity and jealousy. Hopefully these people will find some joy and love in the future.

We don't need to win every battle. Letting losses go makes room for BRAND NEW experiences to come through. Had the comet that hit Mexico's Yucatan Peninsula not have occurred, the dinosaurs could still be ruling the earth. Change happens: let it go.

Don't treat people as bad as they are, treat them as good as you are. Despite the points made above, some things are certainly worth fighting for. If you feel the need to get something off your chest that's important to you, and you've given it proper consideration, do it.

We cannot foresee or control the reactions and response of other people. The decisions that others make are completely their own responsibility. It's up to them to be who they want to be. They may draw closer to us after we've expressed ourselves, or may move further away.

In the long term, if this is something that is desperately important to you, not raising the subject could actually cause you even greater stress. The key message here is not to harbour any ill will or resentment to anybody.

THE WONDERFUL 'ANTI-STRESS' BUTTON

"Things turn out best for the people who make the best of the way things turn out" JOHN WOODEN

Our brains have developed to such an extent that we are now the most intelligent beings (that we know of) in existence. Evolution has taught us the fight or flight response, which has been fantastic for all our predecessors. It is without doubt helpful to have quick mental and physical reactions if you are about to be consumed by a predator.

Nowadays most of us are not in danger of wild animals although in some parts of the world this risk still exists. This underlines the fact that whilst we may view ourselves as modern humans our previous ancestral genetic links are still within us today.

In our busy modern lives, with so much going on, predators have been replaced with other stressful factors. Deadlines, exams, traffic, and work problems are just some examples. Today, the flight or fight response remains, and is controlled by our adrenal glands pumping hormones around the body when we feel threatened.

Sometimes we cope exceptionally well whilst we ride our big and busy waves. On other occasions, however, we are left flapping around in a mountain of 'to do' lists. If we're not careful, this can drain our enthusiasm, creativity and happiness.

Throughout evolution, it has proven successful to remember situations and repeat previous reactions swiftly. Unfortunately our brain has a tendency to overwork to protect us. Our fight or flight system does not switch off easily (it's overworked), so we need to make a conscious decision to switch it off.

If we don't switch it off we end up with *STRESS!*

Don't worry help is at hand. There is a new method that has been proven to help with stress and it is gaining momentum in many large businesses. Some businesses are so impressed, that they are providing special quiet rooms where employees can go to de-stress.

It is a method that has been around for centuries but is really only beginning to gain real traction in the western world. It's a spin on meditation, derived directly from 'age-old' Buddhist principles called mindfulness.

Mindfulness is simply based on taking a pause and concentrating on your breathing. However, when practising mindfulness, you don't think a single thing (or a least that is the gist of it). In practice, thinking nothing is actually quite difficult until you get used to it. Little thoughts come in and out like shooting stars. Some thoughts get stuck in there and so you roll with them, others are in, out and quickly gone. One thing that is for sure is that thinking nothing takes a bit of getting used to. You will fail repeatedly, but you will also get better at it with repetition.

Aiming to stop your thoughts is similar to turning off a water tap. The first few turns may not do it, but eventually, you know the water will stop. Likewise, your thoughts will become fewer as you keep returning to focus on your breathing.

Please find a simple way to practice mindfulness...

Sit in an upright position and concentrate for approximately one minute on your breath coming in and out of your nose. Be aware of where your head, arms and body are touching the chair, where your feet are on the floor and breathe. That's it - simple! Closing your eyes is optional, it's completely up to you. Some people slowly count from one to ten, whilst breathing in and out, and then reverse the process, counting backwards from ten to one. Others like to repeat the word 'relax' breathing in on the (re) and out on the (lax). Personally I just like to focus on my breath coming in and out.

We are all different so please try all three to see which you prefer. Simply focusing on breathing will eventually bring you a real sense of personal peace in a very busy world.

You may want to try this exercise for longer, if so go for it, but I would advise that you take one-minute exercises regularly while you get used to the experience. You can always extend your minutes of tranquillity as you develop.

I understand that there is scepticism about mindfulness, but I practice it and feel it genuinely works. Scientific studies report that it helps with general happiness, sleeping routines, and accurate decision-making.(6) You will find your own rhythm of when to follow the exercise, though whenever you feel stress building, it is a good time.

You might want to try pausing for one minute every couple of hours during the day, (definitely as soon as you feel any stress or anxiety coming on) but also perhaps mid-morning, mid afternoon or perhaps just before you get home from your college, school or workplace.

After a few sessions, you will start to feel stress leaving your body. This happens automatically, as soon as you start to focus on your breathing. Try this for a week. After the first two or three days, you will improve and look forward to your next moment of relaxation.

It may help, at first, to set your calendar to give you reminders throughout the day.

If you're in the office, you may want to slip to the rest room or a quiet space for just 60 seconds of breathing peace. You can do this exercise walking or sitting, and almost anywhere at all. It may help to close your eyes, but this is not necessary (particularly if you're walking).

With time you will notice that you have a genuine little place you can go to that allows you some real peace. You will temporarily become the observer rather than the doer, which will help you to draw back from a situation and see it more clearly. With time and regular practice all the negative self-chatter will go quiet and you will feel joy and contentment flood in.

If this happiness task appeals to you, I recommend reading the book Mindfulness that was co-developed by Professor Mark Williams of Oxford University and Doctor Danny Penman. Alternatively, there are some very good modern day apps out there such as Headspace.

HAS THE BLACK DOG COME BARKING?

"Depression often lies to you"

Like a rainy day, or the biting cold of winter, eventually depression will pass. You may be stuck in a storm right now, but this moment will blow over and the sun will always shine again. You will be stronger, more able, more experienced, and significantly more insightful.

All of us will be hit with a very testing time at some point in our lives. Inevitably, we will all lose family or friends and experience difficult jobs and stress of some description. I have lost friends and family, in some cases very tragically. I have also experienced short periods of low moods like many others. On one occasion, I visited my doctor and explained my situation. This was what I told him:

- I had a sales position in a swiftly declining industry.
- I was still detailed to find new customers, even though many were going out of business.
- Existing clients were unfortunately struggling to pay their bills. Their livelihoods were under pressure. Meanwhile sales staff had to personally visit clients to obtain money: a horrible experience.

- At the same time, I was renting a semi-detached house with two children, a new baby and two large dogs
- Most of the semi-detached house was being used as storage, as we were also building a new house
- Effectively, we were all living in one room too

The doctor laughed and told me, "If I had to do your job I would be depressed." I laughed along with him, but importantly, he advised me to return in two weeks if I still felt low. This is a crucial period, so if you are in a low mood for more than two weeks you must tell your doctor.

We all feel a little down sometimes, it's a natural part of life. Some say our happiness is linked to our genes, our experiences or our circumstances. Whatever we are presented with, all we can do is work on our response. However, sometimes no matter what we do an exceptionally stressful situation may overwhelm us. It is at this time that a visit to your doctor may be worth considering. This is particularly true if it's stayed with you for a couple of weeks. Depression is an illness just like a broken bone and your mind may need medical help.

Depression can sometimes lie to us and create negative self-chatter in our minds, which we then believe.
Lee H. Coleman, Ph.D., ABPP, a clinical psychologist and director of training at the California Institute of Technology's student counselling centre says:

"Not only does the illness make our thoughts more negative, but it tends to make us see negative events as internal, stable and global"

Many successful politicians, including significant leaders Abraham Lincoln and Winston Churchill, actually suffered from depression. Winston Churchill called it the black dog (hence the title of this chapter). I like to think that because these great men suffered from depression, it made them more empathetic to the world around them and gave them insights that other politicians over looked.

The same could be said of many famous actors. Jim Carrey, Catherine Zeta Jones and Brooke Shields have also documented their battles with depression. Perhaps this has assisted them in portraying their characters and connecting with their audiences in more meaningful ways.

Depression hits all members of society: gardeners, painters, bankers, bakers, singers, policemen, wives, plumbers, and farmers. Absolutely anyone can become depressed. Depression is on the rise in our society, but with the correct treatment, it passes.

Another well-known fact is that depression can lie to you. When we are stressed, hungry, tired, hungover, suffering from illness, or not eating well, your thought processes are hindered. You are more likely to view things incorrectly and more likely to see a negative outcome.

If I'm ever ill or overly tired, I try not to think too much, as I know I might make a bad decision. Depression is far too complex to cure purely through correct nutrition, but there is a chemical link between food and the brain. Eating well is vital when we are challenged. Our brains need nutrients, just like our bodies, so a well-balanced diet including protein from meat or fish but importantly including nuts, seeds, carbohydrates and plenty of fruit and vegetables is helpful. A car won't work without the correct petrol and your body needs the correct nutrients, too.

> We are the most intelligent species on the planet,
> yet we pay to live here???

This is just a personal view, but I believe we need to ensure we hold on to specific paths for human contentment and happiness. We have evolved into the most intelligent species on earth, yet much of what we have done has revolved around the race for material gain.

Have we really got it right when all other animal species have a free existence roaming in tight large family groups? We did once live like this, and in some places, we still do.

Nowadays new groups replace family groups at university and workplaces. These are often target driven environments, where earning money or succeeding is the main goal. There is nothing wrong with competition, it is the foundation of business and of human nature. This is encapsulated in Darwin's theory of 'the survival of the fittest'.

I am not suggesting that a capitalist society is wrong, but it can be stressful. Instead of chasing our dinner through a forest, we now chase money through large cities. Some companies really look after their staff and care for them. However, regrettably others may not care enough. So the message is quite simple: happy staff deliver far more for their company than unhappy staff. Make sure you work for a company that looks after and respects its workers. If it doesn't, leave, there are plenty of companies that do.

I sometimes wonder if depression is a backlash against the fast-paced material world that we now live in. Material wealth is very nice, but it's not a guaranteed route to happiness.

You must make sure that warm and friendly people surround you. They may be family, colleagues or friends, all who have our best interests at heart. This love and kindness costs us nothing, and is invaluable. Take a minute to ask yourself, who are the people I really connect with best? These are the people you need right now, and with modern technology you should be able to communicate with them. If it is someone from your past, who unfortunately may not be with us anymore, you can imagine what he or she would be telling you right now.

Depression and bad thoughts are not a crime, get them off your chest and keep talking. Your true friends will help you. If you need a little uplift, or confidence booster, ask your true friends to highlight your strengths. You are a good person and if you're struggling, good friends will always help. Your friends give you an outlet. However, if you feel you haven't got this support, there are organisations such as the Samaritans, which are there to help. This excellent organisation is available at the following website www.samaritans.org. It is always there to assist at times of need.

If you do ever suffer from depression, please realise your bad thoughts are not the real you. A thought is just a thought, full stop! Deep in your heart, you know the real you and these stupid bad thoughts are not even close.

It may be a daily battle, but these thoughts will pass. You will appreciate beautiful bird song again, be astounded by a starry night, see shooting stars, swim in a warm sea, and laugh until your stomach hurts. It's a huge hurricane, a massive storm, but in time it will blow over and you will be back to your very best.

"Success is not final, failure is not fatal. It's the courage to continue that counts"

Winston Churchill

MISTAKES

"I have not failed. I've just found 10,000 ways that won't work" THOMAS A. EDISON

Yes we all make mistakes, but allow me to pass on a fantastic way to look at a mistake:

'A mistake is a blessing... it's life giving you another direction'

Most people are scared to try things because of the fear of failure. However, once you accept the fact that you may fail, trying new things becomes much easier. You can't change the past, so let it go and make a bright future.

Avoid letting your pride get in the way. The more mistakes you make, the faster you will learn. Life loves a trier and some say that if you are not making mistakes you are not living enough.

Make thousands of mistakes, live life to the full. Yes, common sense allows you to eliminate any potential negative issues or to deal with the mines and enjoy the run. It makes things a lot easier and you will make fewer mistakes. In his testimony to the U. S. House of Representatives Al Gore stated, (7)

"As many know, the Chinese expression for 'crisis' consists of two characters side by side.

危机

The first symbol means danger. The second symbol means opportunity."

In the botanical world, nature responds beautifully when attacked by frosty winters. Plants go into hibernation and wait for the joy of spring to arrive. Bushes, shrubs and trees which are pruned in autumn come back significantly stronger the following season. Nature has an internal power to bounce back stronger, and so do we.

Anything can happen, but the response is down to us. Please don't beat yourself up, you can only give something your best shot. Each day is a new day and history is only important if it helps us in the future.

The choice of what we focus on shapes our brain, learn from the mistakes then harness the power of great outcomes and suggestions to improve your life and get back in the race.

If you are looking to reduce your exposure to mistakes in the future, I would suggest taking the approach of Francis Bacon, a renowned scientist and philosopher:

"If a man will begin with certainties he shall end in doubts, but if he can be content to begin with doubts, he shall end in certainties"

THE 80/20 RULE
(Pareto's law)

"Could you make your life easier?"

Good old Pareto was one smart cookie. His principles have been used widely in business and wellbeing. The idea behind Pareto's law is that 80% of results come from 20% of effort.

Vilfredo Pareto was an Italian economist. It's widely reported that he first saw that 80% of the land in Italy was owned by 20% of the population. He then noticed that 20% of the pea pods in his garden had 80% of the peas. He had noticed a pattern.

This principle was then adapted to many situations, which you can see all around you. It may not always be exactly 80/20, it could be 75/25 or 85/15 but I'm sure you get the idea.

Please see a few examples below:
In the home

20% of your home is used 80% of the time
20% of the carpet on the stairs is used 80% of the time

In business
20% of customers generate 80% of profit
20% of the product range generates 80% of the sales

In sport

20% of the football teams win 80% of the time
20% of the players are more influential 80% of the time

In life

20% of your friends give you 80% of the fun and laughter
20% of your friends give you 80% of the grief

What does this pattern mean?

I encourage you to look at your life, to see if you can use this principal to make it any easier or more enjoyable. I have used this principal on many occasions and, given that life is short, it's nice to get to where you want to be as quickly as possible. Please see a couple of real life examples below:

Catch a big fish.

On a beautiful yet very small island in the Pacific Ocean, lives a small group of approximately 60 people with their families. They live an eco-friendly lifestyle, picking a specific amount of fruits and fish to live in comfort.

The children play in the upper most part of the island on a small hill and their task is to look for whales. Once every two months, the children run excitedly down the small hill to let the elders know there is a whale at sea. Immediately, the island's men set off in pursuit of the whale.

If the islanders manage to catch the whale, it means the whole population won't need to fish for a whole month. It's party time for the whole island.

My sales example.

I used Pareto's principal in my first sales job. I recognised that I could be looking for multiple smaller customers, or instead, I could focus on making one big sale. It took a little time, and the pressure was on, but once I caught my first big fish, the rest was easy.

I got a lot of criticism from colleagues for not coming into the office often enough, but to me, that was down time. I was paid to sell and I had to pay a mortgage and feed my family! I had one thing in mind, and that was to look for those 20% of customers who delivered 80% of sales. They were the customers who would keep me well paid and employed.

What I wasn't expecting, was that 20% of the larger companies expand quicker 80% of the time. They opened more stores, so every year, without me even finding new customers my sales would increase. I was the darling of the sales team and I had a chance to help others with their tasks. All of this success came from my dear friend, Vilfredo Pareto.

Job roles.

Certain job roles have set pay ceilings irrespective of how good you are. If you are chasing money make sure you are in a job role that will allow you to earn it.

To return to the fishing analogy make sure that there are plenty of fish in the pond where you are fishing, (a critical mass) I see too many people fishing in ponds where there are minimum fish and too many anglers. Give yourself a better chance use the 80/20 rule and move ponds!

Look at your life. Could you make it easier? Could you allow yourself more time to enjoy life?

- Adjust your calendar to spend more time with the friends who make you the happiest
- Reduce the time you spend with people who annoy you

- Look at the 20% of things that make you stressed 80% of the time and reduce or eliminate them

- Make some space in your wardrobe by throwing out the 80% of clothes that you wear 20% of the time

- Return to places that you love

As you are now aware, it's possible to move forward, following an easier route. This isn't idleness, it's intelligence!

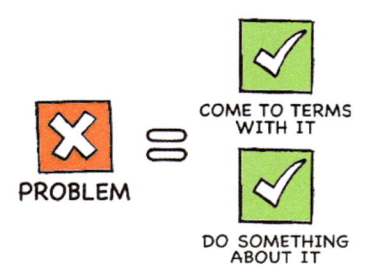

THERE ARE ONLY TWO WAYS TO DEAL WITH A PROBLEM

"Just because something doesn't do what you planned it to do doesn't mean it's useless." THOMAS EDISON

What exactly are your options when dealing with a problem? The answer is simple:

Do Something About It
Or,
Come To Terms With It

Don't torture yourself looking for another answer. I've tried and failed. There are only two ways to solve a problem. There is no third option but you can come to terms with it by changing the way you think about it.

FACING YOUR FEARS

"Courage is resistance to fear, mastery of fear, not absence of fear." MARK TWAIN

Fear can, at times, stop us achieving our full potential. The fear of failure stops many things just a few are mentioned here.

- Asking someone for a date
- Taking a step in a new direction
- Starting a new business
- Taking a trip abroad

My personal fear was public speaking. I'm fine in most social situations, but the simple idea of standing up and delivering a presentation used to horrify me. I remember the day I faced this fear.

I was meant to be assisting the senior management with their presentation, by setting up kits and product displays. The audience was comprised of all the owners and self-made men and women in our industry. In other words, the audience really knew their stuff. The night before the presentation, one by one, the whole team pulled out of the presentation. I was asked to stand in and I was petrified. I spent all night trying to come up with and memorise a speech. After the shortest of sleeps, I tried to remember it again, but my mind was blank!

The speech was due at 10:00 AM. I finished preparing the room at 9:00 AM and then had an hour to remember my presentation. Or at least I thought I did. The secretary told me that the audience would like to see me early. I asked for a five-minute stay of execution.

The following five minutes were full of horror. In my mind, I came up with every possible way out of this meeting. I thought of three options,

- Do a runner (which would have probably meant the sack)
- Pretend to fall ill or faint (which I seriously considered)
- But then a thought entered my head:

"What if you actually managed to pull this off?"

I gave up every hope of this being a good presentation and decided that the main thing was just to get through. I had persuaded myself that I would rather stutter through badly, than walk away. If I walked through that door I could look at myself in the mirror later and smile knowing that I'd tried. The quality of the presentation became a secondary thought and, with that, I walked into the room, determined to do my best.

I did get some positive feedback for the presentation, but this was a secondary benefit. I had just faced my own personal demons, and after the meeting, I was absolutely ecstatic. The feeling of pride in myself was immense. Now I knew something special:

Irrational fear can debilitate you, but it can also be overcome. All you need is a drive and passion to succeed that is greater than the fear.

I look back now and also recognise that part of my response was to look at the worst-case scenario and accept it. For me, this was dealing with professional embarrassment and rejection. If I could accept this possibility, then I could walk through the door, take it on the chin and look in the mirror knowing that I'd tried.

The worst scenario would have been not trying, and that was not going to be the case. The situation also showed me the importance of preparation.

Evolution and facing fear:

Science has indicated that everything we see is made up of the same basic ingredients, Ninety Two elements that are continuously recycled. This applies throughout the known universe; the same elements exist everywhere. Every atom in our bodies was part of something else perhaps a tree, a dinosaur, a rock, or a whale.

So essentially, our elements don't die. We are wonderfully transformed! If the visible universe is one big tumble dryer of particles, some will grow, develop and proliferate because of their environment, and some will decline.

The key words above are 'because of their environment'. Effectively, in evolution, the environment decides the winners and losers. As an example, I will discuss the clever ice monkeys of Japan. There is an area in Japan where approximately two meters of snow falls every day. Nestled amongst this snow lives a group of monkeys. Yes, monkeys. So what are they doing there?

The Ice monkeys have evolved and adapted. They go to local hot spas, where tourists throw wheat into the hot water. The monkeys have learnt to dive to the bottom of the hot spa to claim the wheat. This is evolution in action: ingenuity and perseverance have seen the monkey colony survive and prosper. They have conquered their environment.

The monkeys desire to eat overcame the fear of diving to the bottom of the pool. Remember, to overcome anything all you need is...

'A drive and passion to succeed that is greater than the fear'

Assuming that your reserves of courage have come forth, what else will we need to enhance our chances of facing a fear and beating it?

1) Preparation, Preparation, Preparation

Do your research, until you know everything about your fear. This will assist you greatly in defeating it. The more you know, the less likely it is for something to crop up and push you off the path. Throw any preconceptions and beliefs away and make sure you go with scientific proven facts. Contrary to belief, good entrepreneurs don't gamble. Instead, they make thoroughly studied judgments and then make progress based on facts. This should be your preferred approach.

2) A dry run

If it's ok for skiers, it's ok for us. Films and theatre productions always run many shows prior to a main event, and many times in the past I have made mock up products to gauge feedback prior to a launch. If you get half a chance, practise over and over again. It will increase your chance of success.

3) Commitment

Please read the following two quotations about commitment:

"Whatever you can do, or dream you can, begin it. Boldness has genius, power, and magic in it"
Johann Goethe

"*Until one is committed there is the chance to draw back and subsequent ineffectiveness. But the moment one definitely commits oneself, then Providence moves too. All sort of things occur to help that would never otherwise have occurred. A whole stream of events issues from the decision, raising in ones favour all manner of unforeseen incidents and assistance.*"
William Murray

Put a date in the diary and positively commit to it, giving yourself sufficient time. This will fully engage your mind in planning, and bring together a sense of urgency. Answer every call from your conscious and subconscious about planning (particularly important if this involves finances). Answer every call from your gut feel on getting things thoroughly prepared and right and then when the moment comes pause your worrying brain and confidently progress knowing that you're fully prepared and go for it!

The worst-case scenario is that things may not turn out as you'd expected. Maybe you will fail. Can you handle this?

We are sometimes not particularly good at forecasting our feelings after we have completed something. Humans are exceptionally resilient. We are able to regroup and bounce back after facing problems. I dearly wish people would hold their head up high and take very well considered and calculated gambles (of course it's not a gamble if you've done your research) a little more.

Opening yourself to the real power of vulnerability of getting things wrong is what makes us alive. Those that suppress vulnerability are suppressing joy, happiness and life itself.

One thing is for sure: by facing your fears you will have crossed a bridge that most don't. Be extremely proud of yourself.

YOU'VE TRIED

You've looked your fear straight between the eyes and fought it. Well done indeed.

EXPERIENCING THE BAD, LEADS TO THE GOOD

"The eye only see's what the mind is prepared to comprehend"
HENRI BERGSON

Truth is built on science. Science is built on experiment, observation, and evidence. This is what took us to the moon all those years ago. When we start with certainty, we could quickly be destined for disappointment. However, starting with doubt leads us to test things to find the right way forward. Yes occasionally we may trip up, or go down the wrong path, but eventually this will leads us in the correct direction.

You can't know something until you've experienced its opposite. How would you know:

- When you're happy, unless you've been sad?
- When you're healthy, unless you've been ill?
- When you're in a good relationship unless you've had a bad one?
- When you're in a rewarding job, unless you've experienced an unfulfilling one?

When things are going well for us, everything's great but the biggest lessons we learn are when things just don't go our way and life is tough. These times are what forge our character, make us empathetic with others and give us strength.

These really are life-changing events, so embrace and work through the challenges you face. These challenges are responsible for you finding happiness. Without one, you can't know the other.

One of the best bands the world has ever seen, the Beatles, had a huge hit with the song 'It's getting better all the time'. If you accept this viewpoint, the negative things we experience open brand new doors and pathways for us to make our lives better.

So, why wait until the future to look back and see that everything turned out OK? Don't panic, just work your way through the bad to experience the good once more. Be proud of yourself. Trust me, in time, you will be able to look back and see how strong, capable and resourceful you became.

PROBLEMS, BLAME, ADVERSITY AND CHALLENGES

"Let me tell you the secret that has led me to my goal – my strength lies solely in my tenacity."
LOUIS PASTEUR

Let me be perfectly clear. In life, many things occur which have not been of our making. We may have met outrageous misfortune or we may have been very unlucky indeed. You have my utmost sympathy if this has happened to you and I sincerely wish you well.

I am referring to more day-to-day issues here. When we come up against a problem, what's our first response? We could blame someone else but it won't help us in the slightest.

The blame game just shackles us from progressing and hinders our path. However, as soon as we take responsibility for our problem and accept it, the sooner we can get out of the hole we're in.

Do you ever find yourself sighing and feeling sorry for yourself? Think back to when you began feeling sorry for yourself. Perhaps it's behaviour that you've learnt from somebody else. What you must do is change the word problem in your head to challenge.

There is a subtle difference. A problem suggests that there is something inherently wrong, whereas a challenge encourages us to collect ourselves and take the fight to the next level.

There are no problems, only solutions.

If we can approach any perceived challenges like this, it will encourage our brains to search for answers rather than focus on problems. As previously stated, there are only two ways to deal with a problem: Come to terms with it, or deal with it by thinking about it differently.

Failure

Failure...what a despicable word. I wish it was removed from the English language and replaced with the word adversity. I hate the word failure, as I have given it too much power in the past. This changed when I learnt that there is always another path forward, always another door, always a way out.

It may be difficult to accept, but some say that we should accept adversity as a blessing. It is only in adversity that we learn our best lessons. Sportsmen know this only too well, from the thousands of free kicks that sail over the bar in football training, to the thousands of falls that ice skaters endure when practising a triple jump. These athletes are not deterred by adversity. They know that if they keep trying, they will eventually succeed.

The American electric light bulb inventor, Thomas Edison, would not accept failure he reportedly once said:

"I have not failed. I've just found ten thousand ways that won't work"

You may not realise, but I guarantee that you have it within you to find another way forward. I am amazed by how much strength and power people can demonstrate in the face of adversity. I particularly like the following quote from Elisabeth Kubler-Ross, a Swiss-American psychiatrist:

"The most beautiful people we have known are those who have known defeat, known suffering, known struggle, known loss, and have found their way out of the depths. These persons have an appreciation, a sensitivity, and an understanding of life that fills them with compassion, gentleness, and a deep loving concern. Beautiful people do not just happen"

How can you empathise with people if you haven't felt their pain? How can you understand if you haven't been there? When things don't work out, it's not the end of the road. It is simply the end of one road. There are plenty of others, and it's time to colour in your next exciting path.

Distraction

Although this is not applicable to all situations, you may find that distraction will buy you some precious time to help you to decide which path to take. I like to distract myself from some types of issues. Doing so helps me to think about the problem at hand over a longer time period, rather than finding an answer immediately.

Distraction is not the same as giving up. It gives you time to weigh up all the probabilities and get a gut feeling for your path. Go for a walk. Have coffee at a friend's house. Play a sport. Listen to some upbeat music. Try anything that might raise your mood. You will feel better and, if it's a minor problem, this distraction may give you a better perspective, allowing you to let it go.

Sometimes a problem can be resolved by brainstorming positive and negative outcomes. Try to look at your problem from many different perspectives, taking the time to study each one and challenging yourself to think differently.

The more aware we are of what we are working with, the better our insight and judgments will be. The more you focus on something the more you see, so give yourself time.

Your ability to come up with acceptable or great solutions is directly tied to your capacity to be inventive and imaginative.

It often helps to do something else while your brain is filtering and analysing. I prefer to go for a walk rather than sitting down, it allows me to think more clearly.

You may even want to score each point if it helps, adding all the points up at the end to find a grand total and therefore indicate the best course of action. I know some people that do this very helpfully on an Excel Worksheet. Playing with these inputs helps them to see more clearly and objectively. I have tried this myself and found it very helpful.

Once you have practiced these logical steps, the path forward should be perfectly and abundantly clear. However, if not, and something inside is still nagging you, don't be afraid to listen to your gut instinct either.

If you've weighed all the options up and considered them carefully, but your gut instinct is telling you something else, I might be inclined to go with your gut instinct. I have ignored my gut instinct in the past and been wrong when something I hadn't considered cropped up. I couldn't verbalise, write down or even think to myself what was wrong, but it just felt wrong so I went against my gut instinct. It turned out to be the wrong decision. I should have trusted it. Sometimes you just know the right way forward but just can't put your finger on why.

> *"Follow your heart and intuition they*
> *somehow know the way to go"*

Steve Jobs (Apple founder)

Importantly, don't rush. Give yourself time, as the more aware we are of what we are working with, the better our decisions.

THE NEWS, SOCIAL MEDIA AND THE TV

"Comparing yourself to others is never going to make you happy"

I like to stay abreast of current affairs. When the Olympics saturated our TV stations every night in London, I felt a huge positive surge.

The daily news broadcasted the athlete's achievements, and any other news received a very small window at the end of the programme. I had a very keen sense of wellbeing during the 2012 Olympics.

This taught me a valuable lesson. I, along with the rest of the country, had been immersed with a daily sea of happy faces picking up winning medals after facing very tough tests in the athletic world. When the news reverted back to its normal state of bringing us negative news events from around the world, I was staggered by the change in my mood.

What had happened to me? I asked others and they felt exactly the same. What had happened in those wonderful four weeks when all we had heard was good news?

I knew the power of positive thinking from experiences in my own life but this cemented those beliefs.

All the channels during this month had broadcasted the Olympics. Negative news was only briefly mentioned and was noticeably brief. In our own lives, perhaps this is a model of how to keep our spirits high.

It taught me to be wary of what I'm looking at, particularly the news. There is so much good in the world and yet the bias in the news is so often negative, with news channels competing to show us the most shocking events.

Yes I believe we need to be aware of current affairs, but my advice is to restrict your digestion of the news. You need the positive things in life to overwhelm the negative news and not the other way round.

This also applies to social media, but much further afield too. If we're not careful, too much exposure to social media can lead us into the dreaded and depressing comparison. Comparing yourself to others is never going to make you happy. The only person worthy of comparing yourself to... is you!

Doing the best you can possibly do for yourself and the rest of humanity is the goal. Anybody else's reflections, opinions, successes or failures should not be compared to your own. You're in charge of your own life and comparing yourself to others is not going to help you. It is completely fruitless, unproductive and negative.

Social Media – I welcome the wonderful benefits of social media and its ability to keep us connected. I also sincerely hope that this adds and does not detract from our happiness.
Social media is still a relatively new phenomenon and its impact is still relatively undetermined. Ask yourself: does it add or subtract from my happiness? If it's not adding or uplifting you, try to limit your exposure or delete your social accounts.

Real, face-to-face meetings with close friends and family will always be the best way to communicate and understand people.

TV – I must confess, I love watching TV, particularly when I can record my favourite programmes. I'm sure that in your personal quest for happiness, you've also recognised that it's best to focus on upbeat, positive news stories. The TV can be viewed in the same way. Try to watch the positive uplifting programmes, as this can really assist in raising your mood.

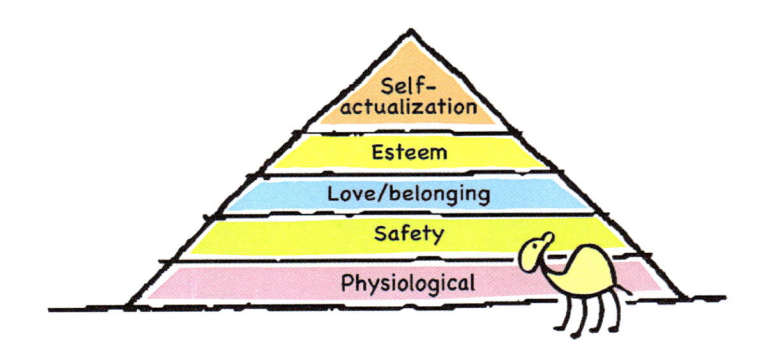

MASLOWS HIERACHY OF NEEDS

"Be happy with what you have, while working for what you want" (HELEN KELLER)

Abraham Maslow (1908 – 1970) was an American psychologist who suggested that all mankind experiences certain needs. Once met, one can then move on to the next level of existence.

A pyramid is often used to highlight these needs, as shown above. The idea, is that all people begin at the bottom and work up to the top of this pyramid. Sometimes, of course, it isn't easy and we may drop a few levels before progressing again.

There is no success or failure attached to the pyramid, it is there to help you to identify more clearly your goals and to make decisions.

Maslow believed that people who reach the top of the pyramid most frequently enjoy 'peak experiences'. These experiences are those when one feels extremely happy and joyful and in harmony with their surroundings.

So in a little more depth, let's see Maslow's hierarchy:

1) **Physiological needs.** This is the first level, best described as needing food to eat to remain alive.

2) **Safety.** We need a roof over our head to keep us warm and we need to make sure we are away from predators so we can sleep soundly at night.

3) **Love and belonging.** Maslow proposes that we need to feel part of a group. We need friends, acquaintances and family in order to feel loved and wanted. This could be as simple as joining your local club, where you will regularly meet people.

4) **Esteem.** Once our basic needs are met, it is nice to feel confident by feeling that we are doing a good job and are successful in what we are doing.

5) **Self-actualisation.** Finally, and when all of the above are met, there may be an inherent need within us to help and share our experience with others. This is not for personal gain, but for the benefit of others.

My understanding of Maslow, is that he thought we should become everything we possibly can, or to become the best that we can be. To look yourself in the mirror and be happy that you've tried to achieve as much as possible.

This could be winning an Olympic medal, being a good parent, or doing well in your profession. Importantly, once achieved and conquered, Maslow believed that real self-actualisation could only be achieved by responding to some even higher goal within your heart. This involved some level of self-sacrifice or spirituality. To reiterate, it was at this level that people frequently enjoy what he describes as peak experiences, to feel extremely happy and joyful within yourself and in harmony with your surroundings.

CONTAINING WORRY

'Logic takes you from A to B but imagination takes you everywhere' **ALBERT EINSTEIN**

One of the basics of mental health is containing or beating any worrying thoughts you have. Being able to direct and control our thoughts is the key. We are all completely different and respond in different ways. Please also read the next chapter: 'Don't overthink, be happy', for a secondary approach.

We fill our days with self-chatter in the brain and we started doing this from a very early age. It is highly likely that through your life, from being a young baby, you have had persistent thoughts, comments and opinions given to you by your parents, guardians, teachers, friends, colleagues and family.

So are they all correct? I seriously doubt it. Research has shown in the past that 85% of the messages given to children up to the age of 3 is in a negative format. A few of my personal classics from my own parents include:

'Come away from that fire. If you're not careful you'll fall in'

'Stop throwing that. You will have someone's eye out'

'Put some fresh pants on. If you're involved in an accident the nurses will want to see fresh pants'

'You can't do that, people will laugh at you'

'You don't want to join that company. They are really good and will find you out'

Needless to say I didn't fall in any fires, have anyone's eye out, or end up in hospital (with or without clean pants). I also had seventeen very successful years at the company one of my parents thought was above me.

I'm not attaching any blame and I love my parents dearly. It's a part of life that we are stopped from doing what we want to do for our safety. Yet, if we hear too much negativity during our childhood and later lives we could easily feel that we were not overly capable or that something bad may happen.

Such negativity breeds self-doubt. There have been numerous occasions in my early life where I have bowed to some authority, believing them when they told me I couldn't achieve something.

If these negative messages are thought to be truthful, we could end up carrying them around all of our lives. Yes, our guardians got us to this point and we should be very grateful, but now we are independent thinkers. It is the present moments that we can savour, adjusting and altering messages. It is today, the here and now that we are in charge of.

If you have some negative thoughts in your head, there is no need to worry as most of us do. It's actually quite useful at low levels (it stops us doing silly things). However, if it's left unchecked it can run riot, creating troublesome worries.

By challenging your own thoughts and beliefs and then checking their authenticity, you can gain greater clarity. Simply remove or re-frame negativity that causes you to worry or be overly concerned.

Self-employed businessmen often need to pre-empt problems before they happen, yet they also must remain creative and inspirational in order to succeed. Farmers will need to look for the one animal that may be a little distressed and overlook the 99 healthy ones running round the field. The point is, we can sometimes get so trapped in negative thoughts that they can end up arising almost automatically.

Have you ever heard of Murphy's Law? The principle behind this is that:
> '*Anything that can go wrong will go wrong*'

Of course, you may want to disagree and you would be correct to refute this negative quote. Engineer Franz Knoll wrote in the International Journal of Reliability and Safety, indicating that

> '*The introduction of verification and checking procedures can improve structural safety and performance and so prevent the application of the law*'

This is hugely uplifting. It states that if we give tasks the correct amount of attention and apply ourselves, we can achieve our aims without anything going wrong. You can sleep soundly, at last.

Every time we think we fire neurons in the brain, these thoughts create moods and emotions. If we are constantly firing negative thoughts, it is hardly surprising that this will affect our mood.

If you are looking to uplift your mood, start looking at what you are constantly repeating to yourself inside your head, challenge these thoughts, and then put a positive twist on them.

The next time a negative event occurs, learn from it, don't repeat it and if you are constantly blaming yourself, give yourself a break. You're probably ruminating too much and thinking too many negative thoughts.

When I was on holiday in Bournemouth with my parents, aged 14, I asked a girl to dance. She was absolutely beautiful to my young eyes and probably aged around 20. Her answer was just two words long: F-ck off!

Admittedly I was punching above my weight, but it still didn't stop me approaching her. I didn't ask any girl to dance for one year after that incident, in case I got a similar response. I look back now at that experience and see two things:

First, I was brave enough to throw myself into battle to win her heart. I have done similar things through my life on numerous occasions and in many differing fields. They may not have always worked out as planned, but most importantly, I was prepared to take the chance to find out.

Secondly, my response on rejection was far too extreme. Because I was rejected, I had the following thoughts:

- You're ugly
- Your fashion sense is bad (that tweed jacket has to go)
- Your personality is dull
- Your face is too spotty
- You will be a bachelor for the rest of your days

As I grew older and the odd compliment came my way, I gradually learnt that all these thoughts were wrong (well apart from the tweed jacket!) I recognised that my negative thoughts were hindering me. I made a conscious effort to change statements to myself. For example:

'You had better not ask that pretty girl for a dance because she will just reject you like the last one and make you feel even worse'

Became the following:
'I'll ask that pretty girl to dance. If she says 'no', that's not a problem. I'll just ask someone else. If I ask 10 girls, I'm bound to get a 'yes' somewhere.

Of course it never took ten girls before I could find one to chat to or dance with (usually no more than five, actually!)

The point of the above is I was worrying and getting anxious over nothing at all.

If a psychologist was present at the side of the dance floor, he would probably have suggested another mental approach to this event. Psychologists use cognitive therapy to enable people to look at events in differing ways.

One method they use is to ask if your thoughts are correct. Are they based on evidence? As you can see, my thoughts were not based upon any evidence whatsoever. I was just told to f-ck off, without cause. Yet, as a result, my mind ran wild with the incorrect negative thoughts listed above.

Getting upset is not helpful. That's a fact. Finding out the actual evidence behind an event is. In hindsight I can understand the reasons for being rejected. A reasonable deduction was that, as a 14-year-old boy, I was just too young for a 20-year-old girl.

Cognitive therapy challenges you to look at things from another perspective. To not link relatively minor things to major things. This is exactly what I was doing as a result of my rejection.

I got stuck in a bout of what is known as ruminating and incorrect linking. I blew things completely out of proportion. I simply got stuck in a vicious circle of incorrect assumptions.

Be careful and try to grasp the genuine reality of situations and avoid making assumptions. Try to break your feelings down in to facts and definitive evidence, much like a scientist might do in a lab. Write things down, perhaps get a big sketchpad and you can really go to town!

Once the evidence is gained, cognitive therapy suggests you should attempt to look at a problem from a different perspective or reframe it. Given that we all interpret things completely differently choosing the perspective that could help us thrive rather that dive is the best way to progress.

Try looking at things from a different perspective.

Rather than blowing the problem up, look for ways to turn your telescope of thoughts around and make the problem look smaller.

Worries are of course normally generated from problems. Addressing these problems or coming to terms with them are the only two ways forward. Let's face it, unless we've got divine powers sometimes it isn't going to go exactly how we predict. This is why insurance policies exist, to cover against unexpected eventualities.

We live on an amazing planet with wonders abounding everywhere, but of course the world isn't perfect. We can only affect what's in front of us and choose where to put our focus.

I really like the following comments from the International Space Station astronaut Dr Sandra Magnus. The Space Station was advised that for the first time in its history, a larger piece of space debris was about to hit and they didn't have time to adjust its orbit. Dr Magnus was advised to go to the Soyuz escape pod. The consequences could have been catastrophic, but her comments were as follows:

"It's either going to hit or it's not going to hit, either way worrying about it is not going to help you! All you have to do is prepare everything that you need to prepare so that if it hits you are in the best possible configuration"

It didn't actually hit, but the team did go back to the drawing board and instituted further significant refinements. All we can do is refine the situation if it happens to not work, and keep refining until we get it right.

See the chapter titled 'Problems blame and challenges' to hopefully assist you in working your way through your problems. Most importantly, in order to deal with a problem, you have to get stuck in, be pragmatic and come up with lots of different potential outcomes. Attributed loosely to Einstein and slightly adjusted is the reported quote

> 'Logic takes you from A to B but imagination takes you everywhere'

The more you focus on something, the more you will see, so get exceptionally creative in solving your problems. Worriers are sometimes focused too much on a problem and not enough on the solution. Simply changing your focus is the first step to defeating any worries.

Once you adopt a problem-solving attitude, you are on the way to reducing your worries. You might want to try cutting the negative chatter and replace it with more uplifting phrases:

'It doesn't matter what life brings, I am exceptionally creative in looking for new pathways. Once I sit down and have a little rest, I can open my mind up to multiple new possibilities'

Here are a few ideas to help you change your perspective or to adopt a better cognitive position:

- Think of time in the past when you have come across a similar situation. What did you do then to get through it? Use that additional courage or confidence as a reminder of your past success. You can call on that pride to give you success again.

- How would one of your heroes approach this situation? I have a few heroes in my life and if I asked them, they would all approach things differently.

- For a bit of distraction, go do some things you enjoy. Go visit a good friend and have a laugh. Then, come back to your worry from a happier position. You will be amazed at how more creative you will be.

- If you're thinking gloomy thoughts or outcomes, try thinking of how your best possible self would cope.

- What were you worrying about this time last year? Can you not remember? Is it highly likely that you won't be worrying about the current problem in a year's time.

- Are there definite links between the things you are concerned about or are you putting 2 + 2 together blowing things up and making 5?

Remember, it's not the event that occurs but our reaction to it that matters. Have faith in yourself, you've survived for this long, and although you may not be able to see it just yet, there are many more good times to come.

DON'T OVER THINK BE HAPPY

"Row your own boat, run your own mile, climb your own mountains, conquer your own goals".

Of course we need to consider things, but if you're anything like me (naturally curious), you may need to stop yourself thinking too much sometimes. Otherwise, your mind can run riot!

Yes, overthinking (or rumination) may be bad for us.[8] In my business life, I have had to think of various possible steps and potential outcomes before they happen. This allows me to cope with them when and if they do. If I hadn't done this, it would have been negligent.

I am also fully aware, though, that too much of this thinking can cause stress. Psychologists call it 'rumination'. Yes we need to consider important things carefully, but if we are not careful, this can creep into everyday life. The result can be that we over analyse everything.

I have found that a priority to where I put my thinking has benefited me, as I am a natural over-thinker. I still accidentally bump into situations that I over-think but have taught myself (often after the event) to let it be. I believe we never stop learning from our mistakes.

In truth, overthinking can be very depressing and have a real downward effect on our moods. We can even end up grasping at scenarios that simply don't exist, but is it really worth the effort? We can end up asking ourselves lots of similar questions, as our brain drops into the paralysis of analysis. What does that mean? Why did they say that? What if this? What if that?

Another good way of beating over-thinking, is avoiding the triggers that make you over-think, in the same way that an alcoholic or habitual smoker might avoid temptation by avoiding easy access. This way you can formulate a plan to avoid circumstances that drag you down this path. Doing something completely different, going down a different road, engaging in a different activity, or visiting somewhere else could help you avoid any traps.

For example, it might be that repetitive comments from someone that you know may be harming your confidence. Avoid contact as much as possible, take pity on them, and forgive them. You're worth much more, and if appropriate, put a smile on your face to demonstrate that their words have had no impact. Don't be trodden on, and if something needs to be said, get it off your chest. It's your choice, but please don't spend your days contemplating what others may or may not think about you. It's only your opinion that counts, as we discussed in the chapter two. Some people are on a different wavelength please just accept that.

I have a personal system in place of 'three strikes and you're out'. This stops me being taken for granted. We all have a bad day sometimes, so I am more than happy to let someone have a couple of bites at me. If they hit three, watch out for the explosion!

Don't compare yourself to others, either. This is exceptionally depressing. The only people's opinion in the whole world that matters is yours.

> Row your own boat, run your own mile, climb your own mountains, conquer your own goals.
> Take pride in your own achievements: these are the only ones that really matter.

So if you find yourself overthinking, consider the things you commonly over think and devise a plan to avoid going there in the first place. Overthinking is bad for you. Replace it with an uplifting activity, or consider regular breaks, using such techniques as mindfulness as described in the chapter 'The Wonderful anti-stress button'. Remember, you are now actively controlling your brain and taking it where you want it to go and NOT where it will idle or drift to.

Part 3
ENJOYING LIFE

GRATITUDE

"Do not spoil what you have by desiring what you have not; remember that what you now have was once among the things you only hoped for." **EPICURUS**

Yes I know some of you may think gratitude is a wet subject, but trust me, it is a great friend to turn to. Yes, the age-old adage passed down through generations 'count your blessings', really is exceptionally beneficial to you.(9) In her book the How of Happiness as Sonja Lyubomirsky describes gratitude as follows

It is wonder, it is appreciation, it is looking at the bright side of a setback, it is fathoming abundance, it is thanking someone in your life, it is thanking God, it is literally 'counting blessings'.

Many psychologists now recommend practicing gratitude. This is because, as humans, there is a tendency among us to become accustomed to the things around us. This is referred to in academic circles as 'hedonistic adaption'. The concept is based on the fact that, after a period of time, we become accustomed to significant positive and negative life changes. For instance, the new car, new clothes or new relationship tend to lose their importance. We simply get used to them. That is, of course, unless we get some level of perspective and balance. This is where gratitude comes in, and it is so important. Gratitude does not imply that we should be less ambitious as ambition and dreams are healthy. Gratitude is simply intended to help us appreciate the things we already have in our lives.

If we are not careful, we could spend our lives on a materialistic treadmill, chasing bigger and better things all the time. In fact, what we wanted only a year ago (or even less) was 'exactly what we have right now'.

There are multiple ways to show gratitude, from writing things down daily or weekly, to talking to people and complimenting them. I would suggest starting a gratitude list or journal on a designated night to begin with, but if you feel the desire to do it more often, then please feel free. There are no rules here, as we are all different. The key thing is to make sure you do it.

When I started to understand the concept behind this simple idea, I found myself walking around daily, looking for things I really appreciated. You can cover so many topics with your approach to gratitude, from managing to catch a train just in time, to being proud of the country you live in. You might feel thankful for your health, or your family. The options for gratitude are endless, let your mind wander and you will find joy in the smallest of things! With time, this is proven to raise your mood and increase your happiness levels.

Gratitude has also been found to reduce tension, allow better sleep patterns and improve your kindness and generosity. If you work on this regularly with practice, you should be able to counteract any negative thoughts with more positive ones and generate a new positive perspective on life based on an attitude of gratitude.

KINDNESS

"Kindness generates more kindness, which makes the world a better place to be"

In a modern competitive society, we are increasingly prone to follow Darwin's theory of survival of the fittest. This, after all, is how we progress, isn't it? Well no, not really. Darwin also suggests that we need to look after the group around us, and show empathy towards others. If we don't, we could be ostracised or rejected.

Being genuinely kind does not just help others. It also helps you. It gives you a boost of feel-good hormones like oxytocin. Darwin wrote in his book 'The Descent of man':

> "Natural selection promotes sympathy, social feeling, unselfishness, and even self-sacrifice" (Darwin)

We are, in other words, hard-wired to take care of others. Some of us, however, may be more genetically prone to this due to the empathy we have embedded in our genes. Yes, some people really can pick up on other people's feelings more easily than others.

Christine Carter, executive director at the Greater Good Science Centre (UC Berkeley) says the following:

"I've found that parents who start consciously cultivating gratitude and generosity in their children quickly see how much happier and more resilient their children become...What is often surprising to parents is how much happier they themselves also become."

So there we have it. Kindness generates more kindness and subsequently increases our happiness. This is also contagious and can spread like wildfire, creating a really positive spin.

Why not try and spread a little warmth, kindness and subsequent happiness to others by doing five kind things in one day, once a week. You may want to do more, and if you do, that's absolutely fine. However, if you do it once a week you can plan it more mindfully.

I'm sure you are a kind person, and would probably do kind things all week, this is absolutely fine but some studies suggest if you want to up your benevolence putting it all into one day really helps you get a lift too.

There is a wonderful statement in the 2007 film Evan Almighty:

Question - How do you change the world?

Answer - "one single act of random kindness at a time"

If it helps, here's a little list to get started, but I'm sure if you sat down for 15 minutes you would be able to create a lot of personal ideas yourself:

- Give someone a bit of your time and let him or her express themselves while you listen
- Buy an unexpected gift
- Weed someone's garden
- Smile at someone

- Give someone a phone call and ask him or her how they are doing
- If its snowing, clear an older persons drive way, or ask if they need anything from the shop
- Leave a tip
- Take some chocolates or flowers to people who you bump into regularly, your teachers, your gym trainers, the person who serves you coffee or the people at the local shop or supermarket
- Be exceptionally courteous to phone callers or door-to-door salesman who have to earn a buck somehow
- Help someone at work with a task
- Help someone at home with a task
- Cook a meal or do some tidying
- Take someone out for a meal or a coffee

Be creative in your kindness tasks and rotate them regularly. It will be good for the recipient and will leave you with a nice feeling too.

GET OFF YOUR BOTTOM

"No drug ever invented can deliver the vast benefits that exercise can"

Do you know of the massive benefits that can be gained from getting off your bottom and moving? You don't need to be a gym addict either: just a simple brisk walk will do you so much good.

The minimum recommendation is for approximately 30 mins of exercise five days a week. That said, obviously any exercise is good for you and even a swift 10-to-15 minute walk around the block can raise your mood significantly.

It can feel freeing, and there are so many benefits. There is no drug in the world that comes close to the benefits that exercise can bring you:

- A reduction in stress levels
- A marked lowering of anxiety
- A scientifically proven reduction in depression
- A noticeable rise in self-esteem
- Better sleep patterns, resulting in a healthier body and mind
- A better cardiovascular system (strengthening your heart)

- Improved energy levels
- Lowering blood pressure
- A reduction in cancer risk
- The improvement in muscular posture and strength
- The strengthening of your bones
- The reduction in fat on your body
- The improvement in your general appearance
- The raise in natural endorphins that make us feel happy and reduce the perception of pain, with no nasty side effects

You may even want to consider the latest trend in exercise: Fast exercise. All is revealed in the excellent book on the subject Fast Exercise, developed by Michael Mosely and Petta Bee. The idea of fast exercise is quick bursts of intense training broken up with longer rest periods. This has been shown to be highly effective when you have a limited time. There is also some excellent free information online about this at fast-exercises.com

Exercise makes a statement that you are in control of your body. This leads to a feeling of wellbeing that can stimulate your confidence and lead you to better control other events too. So as the title says 'get off your bottom' and start moving!

EXCUSES FOR STOPPING PROGRESS

"I attribute my success to this - I never gave or took any excuse." **FLORENCE NIGHTINGALE**

I myself have been guilty of this on many occasions, so please understand that there is no judgement here. We put off many things in our life for reasons that we claim to be genuine. However, are these really genuine reasons, or are we just telling little white lies to ourselves to avoid progressing to a new and better place?

We think of the future, but your future starts today, in the present moment. The future will not just happen the way you want it to without you starting to act on it today.

Young people have dreams of the future, which is great, because we need those dreams at any age. But how many start on the path to making them happen? Some older people look back with regret with words like "If I was young again I'd have done it differently".

You should never have regrets. Above all, never stop dreaming. Instead go boldly forward and make things happen. I cannot emphasise this enough. The ability to believe in yourself, learn from your mistakes and keep going is what creates success.

In my experience, intelligence, money, background, age or gender does not separate winners from losers, what separates them is:

'The ability to make things happen, to not be beaten, and to keep trying.'

My personal story was one of wanting my own business. I wanted to be my own managing director, so I began saving up until I had enough money to launch my own business. I classified this as building my business pot.

The first three business ideas that I tried didn't work brilliantly. I earned a little but not enough to support a growing family. I also recognised that as soon as the pot ran dry, it was time to move on to something new. I ended up blowing a little hard earned money, but nothing more tragic than that. However, the fourth idea worked very well, which gives me the opportunity to now write this book, something I'd always wanted to do.

So here are some of the classic excuses that people give for not making progress:

Excuse One:
I haven't enough money – I accept that finances are an issue for many people, but it does not have to be like this forever. One way or another you can start saving and get there. It might take a few years but eventually you will get there. You can reassure yourself that you have started your journey, just by putting a little money to one side each week. You might even like the idea of getting two jobs, perhaps evening work in a restaurant or bar. Alternatively, can you cut your expenditure somehow? The idea is to create a surplus, a special pot, and from that you are starting your journey. Cash is the concrete on which a business is built and the more you have of it the more risks you can take.

Excuse Two:
I haven't the time – This excuse is nonsense. These are your well thought out dreams, they are more important than anything else.

Just 60 minutes of work each day could help. Turn off the TV, get up earlier, or log off social media. Somewhere, I'm sure you can find an hour in a day. Have you ever heard the saying that 'to succeed you need cold morning desire'? If you want it enough it will happen, but you may need to face a few cold mornings. I've definitely seen my fair share of these over the years. At one period in my life, I was effectively doing two jobs to get ahead. To my advantage, I slept like a baby most nights!

Excuse Three:
My friends and family would disapprove. Ignore them. If your friends and family support you, as they should, they would back you in your wishes and dreams, whatever they may be. Yes if you want to listen to others and consider their opinions, fine. However, ultimately be completely reassured that this is your life and your decision, not theirs. Don't let them influence you in stopping your dreams.

Excuse Four:
I'm too old or I'm too young – You are never too old or too young. History is littered with successful people, young and old. Take a look at just some examples of these remarkable people:

- At the age of five, Mozart was composing music and already an exceptionally competent musician.
- At the age of 14, Nadia Comăneci was an incredibly successful Romanian gymnast, who scored seven 'perfect tens' and won three gold medals at the Summer Olympics in Montreal.
- At the age of 51, Leonardo Da Vinci painted the Mona Lisa and is considered to have been one of the greatest intellectual minds to have ever lived.
- At the age of 61, Colonel Sanders started the KFC franchise after having a variety of different jobs, such as a fireman and an insurance salesman.
- At the age of 76, Nelson Mandela became President of South Africa from 1994 to 1999.

- At the age of 80, my mum celebrated her birthday by going to work as normal. She is one of England's best travel agents, an absolute inspiration (now 81 and still at it!)

So is age a barrier? No, of course not. You are as young or old as you decide to be.

GET BUSY AND CREATE NEW GOALS

"Change is an essential part of life, if it wasn't we would still be living in caves"

The more you have happening in your life, the more interesting you will find it. If one thing doesn't quite work out as planned, it doesn't matter as you have something else to get stuck into. Staying content and happy is not about how we respond to good things (that's the easy bit), but how we react to bad experiences.

If you only have one pursuit that you really enjoy, what will life be like if it is suddenly taken from you? Some ex-athletes, gold medal winners and footballers suffer a low period after their fast-paced, successful career has ended.

I was once an amateur footballer, playing three times a week. I absolutely loved the game and really missed it once I was forced to stop due to an injury. Fortunately, a kind gentleman invited me to play a game of tennis. The football thoughts quickly became a thing of the past as I engrossed myself in that sport too. Tennis was my new love!

We all like close relationships too, but what if regrettably they are suddenly taken from us? Many people who have lived long lives always seem to have an active social life. Research suggests that the stimulus of meeting, greeting and exchanging conversation is a key part of living a healthy life, particularly in older people.

Evolution has shaped our species and historically we have lived in large groups of family and friends. This has been necessary for our survival to catch food, accomplish tasks and defend ourselves. We are wired to be with other people and not alone. We are programmed to interact. The attitude of those we spend time with can assist us greatly, so surround yourself with positive people.

So unless you already have an exciting diverse range of activities that you enjoy, I would suggest trying a few more.

Perhaps try something completely different, outside of your comfort zone. How do you know you won't like something until you've tried it? My suggestion would be to keep trying as many different pursuits as possible. Please don't repeat the following statement to yourself:

"Oh I've never done that, so I wouldn't be able to do it"

The people enjoying the activity had to start at the beginning at one point. Instead, say:

"I've never done that but that's not going to stop me. Eventually I'll just get better at it"

If we have lots of things we put our time into, losing one activity is going to be a lot easier to come to terms with. If we only do one thing, losing that one activity would have much more impact and we'd inevitably feel a much greater sense of loss.

It's ultimately about finding the right balance. However, don't forget to also enjoy yourself. You will be far keener to do activities if you gain some enjoyment from them.

New Goals – Pursuing new goals is vitally important. We inevitably get used to things and need to press the refresh button to feel challenged and to have aims to strive towards. Conquering small steps and hurdles on the way to bigger goals gives us a real uplift and feelings of accomplishment. Once we've conquered one goal, we must then look for further pursuits, or we may end up feeling stagnant. Trust me, change can be exceptionally motivating and invigorating.

I personally noticed this predominantly at work. Every few years, I desperately needed a new challenge. Sometimes this would be within the existing company and I would move divisions or change job roles, but as soon as I felt I couldn't push the boundaries any further, I knew it was time to move on. If I hadn't pursued a change, my performance would slip and I didn't want that to happen. So I often moved on when I felt I was at the top of my game, as I knew that I couldn't benefit any further. This meant that it was the best time to move, as my credibility was at its highest.

Despite this, if you enjoy your job, it would be madness to change it. Finding that all consuming goal in a profession or career that drives you to rise every morning is an incredibly fulfilling, joyful and wonderful thing to possess. We all need a project, a goal and an aim, because they drive us onwards. Take some time out to find new pursuits and goals, and do your best to master them. If it's possible, try this with others too. Being in an environment where everyone is working towards a common goal is sometimes more sociable and enjoyable.

For me, that current goal is passing on my experiences in the hope that people recognise that they can make a change to improve their lives. I made many changes in my career and sports interests, and was often criticised for it. I now know that the people passing judgement were talking from their own personal experience, not mine. Change is an essential part of life. If it wasn't, we would still be living in caves!

The more you have booked in your diary, the younger and more active you will feel. Fill your diary with things you enjoy doing, but don't forget new goals, new pursuits and to keep busy.

Exercise: Five productive things–
Try choosing the five most productive things you can do at night before you go to bed ready for the next day and list them. Place them in order of priority, and you're ready to go. It may be that you only get the first one or two actions done, but at least these are the most important tasks. Don't feel disappointed if points four and five don't get done, they may creep up the list on another day.

You've done the most important things on your list and you will be amazed how many people do not even consider this. Some days, the number one priority might be having fun all day and relaxing. Sometimes the most important thing to do is crack on through your tasks. By all means, make a larger list than five, but ensure you have listed them in order of priority.

Creating new goals is an investment in your future. You will certainly face challenges, but it will be worthwhile. Bouncing between different tasks, winning and losing, or just participating, will add a real richness and joy to your life.

So begin by writing a list of goals and things you would like to achieve:

1) Write your goals down and make a commitment to yourself to do them. Be upbeat and optimistic: "I can do this"

2) Plan the baby steps you will need to follow in order to achieve your desired outcome or goal. Stick to them. You can always adjust them a little, if required. The idea is to first think it through, and then to take the appropriate action.

You're on your way and should now have a few projects in mind. May I wish you the very best of luck. Once you reach your end goal, savour it, be grateful for it, and then find your next project!

THE AVALANCHE EFFECT

IDEAS CREATE MOMENTUM

YOUR DREAMS ARE YOUR BEST PLAN

"Hunger and ability are the seeds of success, the good news is you can develop both."

You may not realise it right now, but if you ask any older person how fast life goes, they will tell you, 'very quickly'. We can soon get caught up in life: with jobs, houses and family. Although these are wonderfully exciting and marvellous things to do, I would encourage you to make some space and time for your other dreams too.

I always wanted to run a marathon, but when I finally found the time to do it my body refused. My knees had endured three operations from competitive sport and I risked serious damage, so those days were done. I had so much fun enjoying my competitive sporting days that I have no regrets at all, but there is a point here. The marathon dream was not achieved. I had presumed I had the time to do it, but I was wrong.

I have heard stories from older men and many have said that they wished they hadn't worked so hard and had spent more time with their partner and children while they were growing up. If you are not careful, you can be caught on a treadmill of work and miss out on some of the most important things in life.

Make time for yourself to achieve the things you'd like to do. What interests, projects or hobbies could you engage in? Is there something you have always dreamt of doing or achieving? I am a huge believer that if you have a project to embrace, you are a long way down the path to happiness.

Just getting 'on the path' gives you a real lift. It delivers a purpose. Be aware, however, that if the project has a finishing line, you will need to look for another new project once it's complete. You may sometimes find that striving down your path toward your dream is occasionally more fun than the achievement itself.

Some goals and dreams will give you far more lasting happiness than others. A career you are completely dedicated to, for instance, will give you great joy. If you are looking at new goals and interests, choosing ones that will involve you coming into contact with others should assist in uplifting your spirits.

We all chase material possessions to some extent, but do not expect lasting happiness from these purchases. What is really precious, are dreams and goals that are personally meaningful, particularly if it involves assisting others. Take some time out and think about the things that really matter to you. Being focused on achieving these things will fully engage you and leave you feeling more fulfilled.

Time rolls on so quickly, and sometimes we grow out of our circumstances and need new horizons. Don't pay attention to criticism from others just because you need a change. Go ahead and make it. It is your divine right to choose your destiny. You are entitled to make a change.

I love my dad and have immense respect for him, but he has on almost every occasion delivered the following words when I have tried to make a change:

"What do you want to do that for? You've got a problem"

Yes Dad, I do have a problem. I need to feel motivated and engaged in life, and fortunately for me, that's involved making changes (particularly my job roles). It may not be for everyone, but for me, variety really is the spice of life. My dad is a great friend, but we both now recognise that we are completely different, and there is nothing wrong with being different.

Avalanches are very powerful. One small boulder can create thousands of tons of rocks and earth cascading down a mountainside with ferocious speed and momentum. The avalanche is a metaphor for your dreams. Once you take that first step, you can create an unstoppable avalanche of success for yourself.

"If you can dream it, you can do it."
Walt Disney

Acting on your ideas creates serious momentum, so remember that you're only one step away from creating an avalanche effect. Yes, you may have slip-ups, trips and falls, but you will learn from them and get stronger, wiser and progress further each time. Again, this is about taking action, so you must identify the hurdles you may need to jump over to get to where you want to be.

With some careful planning, you should be able to create some freedom in your life; to achieve the things you want to do. Perhaps a less strenuous job, or self-employment, may give you more time. Over the years, I saved money so that I could one day be self-employed. That money has allowed me to enjoy running my own company for six years. It has also generated the time required to help me write this book.

Creating space can give you more time to plan, more time to think and more time to discover your dreams. Live your life in a way that is true to yourself, and not what others want of you. In the end, your dreams are your best plan.

CHANGE

"Action may not always bring happiness, but there is no happiness without action". DISRAELI

Have you ever had the feeling that a change is necessary? No matter what you do, or how hard you try, you just need another challenge? This is a perfectly natural feeling, it's just part of life. Just like a caterpillar turns to a chrysalis then a butterfly, what's correct for you now may or may not be correct in the future.

I have had this feeling creep in for most of my professional life, which explains my very varied career, from farming to IT networks and from being in sales, to setting up my own company.

I used to initially enjoy the challenges, only to discover further down the line that it became a little mundane and I needed to do something else for my sanity. I accept, of course, that some people don't like or need this changing stimulus. I used to work with some excellent administrators who absolutely loved their jobs and took real pride getting things right every time.

Being fully involved, challenged and excited about projects at work is a great feeling to have. Probably self-employment is the nearest thing I have found because there is always another challenge to conquer, or a new product to launch. That said, I would be equally open to working for someone else or another company again, if the challenge felt right.

The fact is, things change. I probably should have jumped ship far more quickly than I often did. Eventually, I got used to the feeling of restlessness within me and knew it was time to go.

When to stick and when to twist?

There is the famous card game statement 'stick or twist' you either keep the cards you have or risk losing it all in the hope of something better. Ultimately, this is your decision to make. If you have the ability and courage to take that choice, go ahead, but I never recommend gambling it all. Always keep some money to one side to give yourself a chance to get back in to the race.

This may not mean just money but also your reputation. Keep your standards as high as possible, but also be easy on yourself if you screw up. We all hit difficult situations and torturing yourself is a complete waste of time. Pick yourself up, dust yourself off and feel fortunate that you have learnt valuable lessons for the future.

Of course we never really lose it all. There's always another day and another avenue, as one door closes, another opens to brand new opportunities.

If you are thinking of changing your job role, do so with your credibility in your existing job completely intact. This way, if everything happens to go pear shaped, you may be welcomed back with open arms. When making job changes in the past, I have always worked exceptionally hard, particularly in the last three months of employment. You never know what's round the corner, so what is the point in burning bridges.

Even if you're not treated particularly well in your final months in a company, keep your head held high and walk out the door with honour. You will then have a higher probability of offers to return in the future and it's always good to keep your options open.

Rather than change companies, you may be in a position to consider a move internally. This offers a new challenge. If, on the other hand, you feel there is still potential in your current role, then you may consider changing how you approach it. If you can reframe it so that you can thrive, then you may not need to make a drastic change. This may be necessary for your immediate sanity in the first instance, while you search for another job.

I also suggest having a two-week window, we all get bad days at work but if you feel the same after two weeks, it's definitely time for action. I used to use the 'baseball system' at work to avoid being taken for granted. If I genuinely thought I had a grievance or had been mistreated in some way, I would mention it twice. If the same problem occurred on a third occasion, I would start looking for a new role. I have used this system twice to change jobs in the past. I've also done the same with suppliers in my business and it has worked very effectively. One thing is for sure, you should never be bored in your work. If you are in need of a new challenge go find it!

It isn't just in our working life that change can be healthy. People change too. We all evolve. We will grow much closer to some people and move further away from others. This is not something to worry about. It is a natural part of life.

I like the following caption based on a quote from Washington Irving who was born in 1783 (14).

> "There is a certain relief in change, even though it may be from bad to worse. I have found when traveling in a stagecoach, that it is often a comfort to shift one's position and be bruised in a new place."

Sometimes things don't work out, even after you've made a change. However, if you are prepared to accept that and risk hurting another area, you are definitely ready for a change. To strive to be the very best you can be is one of the most noble things you can do for yourself and the rest of humanity.

JUST THREE GOOD THINGS EVERY DAY

"If you lead with love and light, good is only going to come out of it" **WILL SMITH'S GRANDMOTHER**

We are all a unique mix of genes, so it's hardly surprising that what constitutes one persons happiness may not work for an others. You may be young and like loud music and excitement. You may be older and appreciate something calmer. Either way, there is scientific research suggesting that we can train ourselves to be happy by logging the daily things that uplift us.

Writing down your high points as they happen or at the end of the day is a great way of reminding you that there are happiness leaps within your day. The principal behind this is to write down a minimum of three good things that happen every day. When you look back at these highlights, the change of focus will create a self-perpetuating positive cycle, which then reminds you of the things that make you happy.

After a period of time, you will have your own personal collection of things that make you happy. The list will just keep on growing. List them wherever and whenever you like. Either way just make sure you do it and after a week (and definitely a month) you should notice an uplift in your happiness.

You then have a personal list to read again and again. Sometimes if we are a feeling a little blue, a happiness diary can remind us of all the good times and fun we've had.

Please don't assume that this means sitting on your backside and ruminating about your contentedness either. Whilst it's healthy to remember good things, it's also stimulating to plan the next great things that are coming. I've being following this exercise for ten years, noting uplifting and motivational sayings that I come across. It is these notes that have eventually been the source and inspiration for this book.

NATURAL HAPPINESS HORMONES

"If we could give every individual the right amount of nourishment and exercise, not too little and not too much, we would have found the safest way to health." HIPPOCRATES

Did you know that 'feel good' compounds (hormones) naturally generate in your body? This wonderful box of tricks can be released in many different ways so let's list a few of these to help you to get a quick natural fix:

The Cuddle Hormone – Oxytocin is known widely as the cuddle hormone. So go get a big hug from someone you like and let those loving hormones run through your body. You'll have the same benefit from doing a random act of kindness for someone else. So that's official, being nice is scientifically proven to make you feel nice.

The Exercise Hormone - Serotonin is generated when we exercise. This doesn't have to be extreme sports. Just a 30 minute brisk stroll can boost your levels. Eating carbohydrates and getting in the sun is also suggested to boost Serotonin levels.

The Laughter Hormone - Endorphins are produced when we have a good laugh and this is great at reducing stress. The levels of cortisol (the stress hormone) are clinically shown to fall when you laugh. Laughing has also been shown to reduce pain and boost immunity. So stick a comedy programme you like on the television or go meet a friend for a good laugh.

The Achievement Hormone - Dopamine can kick in when we get a sense of achievement and are proud of ourselves. By sticking to a to-do list, as I discussed earlier, you'll get this natural kick of pride in yourself every time you can tick a task off. Music has also been shown to generate dopamine, particularly if it's music you really like, so pull out your favourite tracks and enjoy.

NOW I CAN SEE YOU

"To the world you might just be one person, but to one person you could be the world" BILL WILSON

Being closely connected to others is one of the most wonderful things in the world. Knowing that someone accepts you, warts and all, is exceptionally uplifting and should be treasured.

It may be your family, your friends or partner, but given time, you will find people who will know and trust you at the deepest level. There is simply just a connection. Cherish, foster and treasure these relationships, they are the foundation to your happiness.

Fulfilled people are strong, courageous, understanding, loving, and happy. They will say sorry easily, they will laugh out loud and they will be genuinely interested in the welfare and happiness of others. Being completely genuine and true to yourself will help you to warmly develop these really close relationships.

- Open yourself up and be genuine, it may be a little scary, but this is the real you.

- Love the people in your life, knowing that there are no guarantees that this will be returned. You may be hurt, but the reverse of this will stunt relationships, so do all that you can to create and keep strong bonds.

- Clear the way for some vulnerability it could open new horizons for you. Please don't worry what others think either, that's not your problem, it's theirs. Not being bothered what others think when they see the real you is a sign of real maturity.

YOU

are an exceptional person

JUST
THE WAY YOU ARE

You have nothing to hide. Open up, be true to yourself and it will enrich your life with the people that really matter.

SEEK OUT LAUGHTER

"A day without laughter is a day wasted"
CHARLIE CHAPLIN

Don't we just love a good belly laugh? I have been absolutely floored on some occasions with tears running down my eyes and an aching stomach. We love a laugh, so it's hardly surprising that research suggests it is very good for us too. It's great for stress relief: oxygen floods into your lungs, your muscles contract, your blood pressure changes and your brain releases endorphins.

It is such a good mood changer and can give you a new perspective on problems. Sometimes the best thing to do is leave your problem at the door, go have a good laugh, cheer up, and then address the problem. Once you feel more upbeat, you will have a clearer vision of positive outcomes that you couldn't see previously.

On many occasions, I may have been feeling a little low with minor colds and tiredness prior to a Friday night out. I have pushed myself to go out and socialise, only to find that it's made me feel significantly better. This is no stroke of luck, as laughter hormones help lower the excessive cortisol in our system caused by stress.

Subsequently, our immunity is raised which can help our bodies fight off minor illnesses.

Happiness can also make us feel more connected with other people, decreasing the chance of low moods and depression. Studies carried out in the Framingham Heart Study(18) indicated that happiness was contagious, with someone's good mood tending to rub off on their companions. The effects were powerful, and the conclusion drawn was:

> People's happiness depends on the happiness of others with whom they are connected. This provides further justification for seeing happiness, like health, as a collective phenomenon.

So, if you want to feel a little happier, build your social connections wisely and spend more time with upbeat positive people. Importantly, remember the importance of kindness and spread some happiness to help raise others moods too.

I WANT TO BE THE BEST

"We become what we think about most of the time, and that's the strangest secret." EARL NIGHTINGALE

Do you want to change your situation and be the very best at something? Let me tell you three simple ways to make this happen.

1. Dedicated meaningful practice, and up-to-date research
2. Dedicated meaningful practice, and up-to-date research
3. Dedicated meaningful practice, and up-to-date research

I really like a quote loosely based on an interview with the Arsene Wenger the long serving Arsenal Football club manager.

"It's all possible with intelligence, thought and persistent endeavour, but it won't happen without the graft"

This doesn't entail doing the same thing over and over again (although this may help some disciplines), it involves finding out the latest research, receiving top advice, and accessing the latest equipment. Above all, however, it's about cracking through the hours and maintaining focus.

If you enjoy your chosen subject matter, or it's a lifelong passion, you shouldn't mind this level of input. If you want to be the best, it's exactly what you will need to do. All top masters of their profession started out as novices.

All top sportsmen practise for hours and hours, and as soon as they stop, they fall off the perch. You may notice many top sportsmen around the age of 25 succeeding. It is probable that they have been practising for at least 10 years. They must be absolutely dedicated to their chosen profession, and the rewards of their hard work are finally coming to fruition.

Olympic athletes, footballers, and musicians all have to go through this process. If you really want to be the best, hard work is a major part of the answer.

Good coaching, supportive parents, and facilities also help us to achieve great things. Andy Murray, Venus and Serena Williams, and Tiger Woods were all invaluably supported by their parents when they were young, and thus contributed to their children's success. Despite being blessed with opportunity, it was the hours of meaningful practice that these individuals put in, based on intelligent research that made the difference.

Please understand and grasp that anything is possible. If you really do want to be the best, it simply takes dedicated, meaningful practise, and up-to-date research.

SMILE YOURSELF HAPPY

"We shall never know all the good that a simple smile can do" **MOTHER TERESA**

Of course we smile when we are happy, but did you know that good research points to the fact that we can smile ourselves happy too?(11) We all possess in-built intuitive antennas allowing us to interpret the facial expressions of others and the emotions they portray.

If you see someone smiling or laughing out loud, it promotes a corresponding response in us. Equally, when we see someone who is sad or unhappy, we can empathise with them too.

The theory goes that if we can pick up on the facial expressions of others, we should be able to pick up on the facial expressions we create for ourselves. Your facial expression is likely to trigger the corresponding feeling.

Dr. Robert Zajonc, a psychologist at the University of Michigan states:

"I'm not saying that all moods are due to changes in the muscles of the face, only that facial action leads to changes in mood"

So what can we do with this information? Well, as strange as this may sound, try to smile all the time! When you're on your own, with others, or in front of the mirror. Gradually it will become a habitual mood booster. I started smiling in the mirror after reading the research behind it, and to be honest it did feel a little strange to start with, but with time I grew comfortable, smiling at myself. Now it's the ultimate selfie and it raises my mood!

So if you're under a bit of stress at work or stuck in traffic, try the old adage of 'grinning and bearing it'. Passing on a simple smile to someone costs absolutely nothing and will raise their mood as well as yours.

CATCHING THE 'FLOW'

"To affect the quality of the day, that is the highest of arts." HENRY DAVID THOREAU

Have you ever been so engaged in something that time itself seemed to stand still? You look at a clock and then a little while later you can't believe the hours have flown that fast. Perhaps you're using your entire physical prowess in a sport. You're in the zone and absolutely loving it: nothing is defeating you today!

It might be at work, you're really enjoying your job, it's challenging, but today you are completely focused. You've dealt with everything remarkably well and just right now you feel so utterly capable, proud and pleased with yourself. This is what I mean by 'Catching the Flow'

For me this was achieved on a number of occasions when I played football. One of the early occasions was at the age of 16 when I was playing an American team in a trial game at West Ham United. The incumbent manager at the time was Ron Greenwood, who later progressed to become the manager of the England team.

I was pumped up and wanted to make a good impression. The first occasion I got was when a tricky winger got past our full back and I was dragged out of position to close the player down. I took the opportunity to make a sliding tackle on wet grass. I managed to win the ball fairly, but in doing so took out the player and another man standing on the side lines: the future England manager, Ron Greenwood! Was I in the flow? You bet I was. Luckily, he stood up and shouted "great tackle son, get back in there".

We have all experienced these flow moments, but how can we manage to keep them flowing? Maintaining focus and staying attentive is key. Avoiding all distractions and being totally absorbed by the job in hand will not only mean that you do a better job. It will also increase your chances of catching a flow, 'no matter what the task'.

Some experiences may always get us into a flowing state, a good conversation, playing your favourite sport, doing a task we are really good at. However, sometimes the flow may just not be there and this is the time to take action. So what's the answer?

Some research suggests that the key is to continuously challenge yourself because after a while in the same way we get used to the latest material possessions we can also just get used to doing the same things. As we discussed in another chapter its about maintaining freshness. Finding the mid-ground between being challenged and tested to our utmost capabilities, and then feeling the joy of winning through is not easy. Yet it can be done and is a wonderful feeling when achieved. It doesn't have to be something exceptionally hard, it just has to be something hard enough to really test your present limits. Then when you win through and achieve your desired goal, you'll get a real sense of pride and a wonderful natural rush of dopamine.

You will become more capable and skilled at tasks the more often that you do them. The first time you conquer the task in hand, you will get a real buzz. This may continue for you for some time, but keep challenging yourself to improve in order to constantly get that flow feeling.

If you feel that you're not being tested enough then you need to address the situation or you risk stagnation. Whilst you strive to improve in doing one task, you sometimes need to move to a new subject area where you can begin to master a whole new challenge. The real joy of this is that we become more enlightened, engaged, skilled, and fulfilled. In effect, we just keep on growing and developing as people. So don't be afraid to chase a new task, skill, qualification, job, or hobby. In fact continue chasing them for your whole life!

SAVOUR THE MOMENT

"Slow down you move too fast, you got to make the morning last" **PAUL SIMON**

Savouring is described in the Oxford English Dictionary as the ability to enjoy or appreciate (something pleasant) to the full especially by lingering over it. It is best known by the phrase 'I wanted to savour every moment'.

We often tear around from here to there in our busy lives, grabbing food to swiftly eat without a single thought for its flavour or where it's come from. Eating food can be a wonderful experience if you slow it down and wait for the very distinct and different flavours to hit your palate.

The next time you eat something, just put it on your tongue (something quite small like a raisin or a very small piece of chocolate perhaps). Sit there, close your eyes and wait for five minutes while the rich tones of this small food slowly work their way into your senses. Where has the food come from? What country were the grapes grown in? Where did the cocoa beans come from? Consider how much work has gone in to producing this very small portion of food on your tongue. I think you will be delightfully surprised by how much you could enjoy just one small piece of food. If we can savour food in this way, we can adopt this philosophy to other parts of our lives and extract more pleasure from our day-to-day experiences.

Just as a small piece of chocolate can give us great pleasure, two or three bars would probably make us feel a little sick. We referred to hedonistic adaptation earlier, explaining how we can soon become used to material possessions. It's the same with chocolate. Having a wide variety of things to savour is an excellent way of retaining this pleasurable pursuit.

It is pretty obvious that the more time there is between something, the more we appreciate it. Simply abstaining, or giving it up for a while, drives our appreciation of it the next time we bump into it. In effect, less is more. So don't worry if you are missing something, you are much more likely to enjoy and savour it the next time. There has been much work done in this field and the benefits are widely reported. (12)

Savour the past and the future. Yes, we can savour events from the past and potential events in the future too (using the power of our imagination). Think of happy moments from the past and revel in them as if they were still here. Dream of potential future events and revel in them too. This is not meant to be a chore, but joyous. Use your imagination and enjoy the experience. The more creative you are, the more you will enjoy it.

Part 4
QUICK MOOD LIFTERS

QUICK MOOD LIFTERS

'Sometimes it doesn't matter if the glass is half empty or half full. It's just good to be grateful for the glass and know there's something in it.'

You may sometimes feel a bit down and feel that you need to snap out of it. Thinking the same thoughts or doing the same thing isn't going to move you away from this mood. Good mental health is being able to recognise your mood and to take action if necessary.

Try a few of these actions below to change your mind-set. If you're in a dark place now, you'll probably think there's no point. I'll just feel like I do now. No you won't you will have introduced something different and given yourself a change of perspective, that's what we're doing here changing perspectives to itch you back to a better mood. Research states that if we are in a positive mood, we can envisage better and more positive outcomes.(17) This subsequently begins a wheel of success, which could then lead us to a longer and happier life. We've discussed many different strategies, but knowing something is absolutely useless unless that knowledge is useful. You must first...

PLAN AND CREATE SOME ACTIONS

This is where it all starts: planning.

Variety really is the spice of life. Some people like tennis, some like art, some like football, and some like baking: the list is endless. What would be very helpful for you, is to launch a search for the things that work for you.

Once you have found the things that add to your happiness, make sure you plan these things into your day or week and follow them through. Many people rely on daily tablets to keep them alive. This is how you should approach your happiness. It is vitally important that you get your daily dose of activities, which uplift you and raise your spirits.

Freshness - I know the below works because much has been tested by excellent research, but one thing is very important and that is "Freshness". What I mean by freshness is that as much as I know these things are exceptionally helpful, you have to make the judgement of when to jump to another activity, when to stick, when to twist and when to return to an activity. This is because we are all uniquely different, some will benefit more from different activities than others but keeping freshness at the front and keeping it interesting will keep you engaged.

You are more likely to do things that you enjoy. If something isn't floating your boat anymore, don't fret. Try something else or do it in a different way.

Remember the saying of Benjamin Disraeli the British Prime Minister

"There is no happiness without action"

The things you do, the goals you set, the thoughts you think and your attitude to life dictate your happiness. Determination is also key. It's up to you to decide how and when you start your path to more happiness, but given that this is probably one of the most important things you will do, I suggest you get organised right now. Start with a diary of some description and begin.

Consider how much time you've invested in college or school, how much practice you've put into alternative pursuits like musical instruments, sports or even socialising. Surely, a little time invested in planning your happiness should be a priority?

Everybody, from concert pianists to flight pilots, have had to dedicate lots of time to master their skills. Nobody would have achieved these skills without time, dedication and persistence. Pilots follow given procedures to keep planes flying safely, which is why millions of people fly safely all over the globe each year. Likewise musical orchestras (and bands) have to follow a given set of predetermined musical notes to ensure they are in tune.

It really is hardly surprising that the most wonderful, intelligent organ in the universe, our brain, needs a little guidance to push it in the direction of our choosing every now and again. If not, it would be like letting a plane fly where it liked or letting an orchestra run wild.

We are uniquely and consciously aware of our place in the cosmos, and we are capable of deciding and choosing what to think, how to think and what actions to engage in. If we put these actions together correctly we can obtain happiness, if we put them together incorrectly we can significantly hinder our opportunities. Surely planning our happiness strategies should be as key to our existence as brushing our teeth, showering, shopping and exercising, yet strangely it is rarely considered.

There are many names for it, but practising optimistic thinking routinely will eventually become a habit. When it does, it will change you into a brand new person with a great attitude enabling you to live life to the full. Once you're on your way, you will no longer need this book, as these techniques will be engrained into you. Stick this book on the top shelf when you're on your way to positivity and optimism, but feel free to retrieve it in times of need or as a reference.

Your happiness is crucial, not just for yourself but your family and friends too. Happiness is available for everyone irrespective of academic knowledge, wealth or status. It doesn't need to be difficult or complicated, it just needs to be worked on. Starting one happiness task can get the happiness wheel turning until, all of a sudden, you are flying and confident for all the right reasons.

Now, when the storms come, you have a system, tools and weaponry in place to help you to reach significantly brighter days. So grab your pen and paper and select your favourite activities from the list below. Once you've selected the activities that seem to resonate with you, simply start booking these activities into your diary. In all events you engage in, be the very best version of yourself.

> Stand tall and be confident. Love people. Laugh out loud. Spread joy and happiness. Give your friends a hug and keep smiling. You really are very special and completely unique.

Here's the list to follow below. Go grasp some happiness...

Take a pause – Through evolution, our brain repeats patterns of behaviour. Unfortunately, sometimes our brain has a tendency to overwork to protect us. If we don't switch it off, we end up with stress. Sit down in an upright position and concentrate for approximately one minute on your breath coming in and out of your nose: that's it! Do it as regularly as you feel the need to. It works and you will improve with practice.

Listen to music – There is nothing like getting some of your favourite tunes out to get you feeling good. Combining music and exercise is a double hit, but if you don't fancy the exercise, just playing music can have a very positive effect on your mood.

Listening to music has been shown to start a wide selection of cognitive stimuli in the brain so put on those tunes for a quick lift.

Get outside and get off your bum – I saw an interview with one of the oldest gentleman on the planet recently, he was 114 and in remarkably good shape. He took a 30 minute walk every day before breakfast, and lived on a diet of fish, vegetables and fruit. He was in remarkably good shape, and if it rained or snowed he got onto his indoor walking machine and did half an hour of exercise on that! What an amazing man. Take a walk in the park, or even a 10 minute walk around the block. Just getting outside and going somewhere else will give you a completely new perspective.

It's a brand new day – The sun has been rising on the earth's horizon for millions of years now, so we can be pretty certain it will be here tomorrow. However, life is lived in 24 hour sections and all we ever really have is 'the here and now'. Yesterday is history and tomorrow is a mystery. The here and now is everything, so make the most of it while you can and remember to savour and enjoy the journey.

A bit of company – Seek a friend, relative or a perfect stranger, and talk. I love a good chat with a new potential friend. Don't be shy, most people will appreciate a chat if you show some interest in them. I have had great conversations in public places such as trains, planes, buses, hotels, pubs and gyms. It's amazing how a laugh and a smile can raise your mood. The enthusiastic spreading of goodness, joy and fun raises the spirits of everyone.

Karma – Mostly, what goes around comes around. Once we do a genuinely nice thing for someone else, we get a nice feeling inside. Not only that, the favour is normally returned too. It creates a positive circle of good will that just keeps going and growing. Simply spreading love will fulfil you in ways you cannot imagine. Be careful, though, it's a two-sided coin, If we wish others ill, it may come back to bite us.

Gratitude – Consider all the good things that you currently have, even the small things. Count them up and read them regularly.

Practise this with a real sense of appreciation and you will soon raise your mood. There are multiple ways to practise gratitude, from writing things down daily or weekly to talking to people and appreciating them. I would suggest starting a gratitude list or journal on a Sunday night at the end of the week to start with, but if you feel the desire to do it daily then please feel free. There are no laws here as we are all different but the key thing is to make sure you do it.

Embrace those things that you have and you may eventually develop a whole new way of looking at life.

Catch the flow - Have you ever been so passionately engaged in enjoying or doing something that time itself seemed to stand still? You look at a clock and can't believe the hours have flown that fast? This is what I mean by 'Catching the Flow'.

Avoiding all distractions and being totally absorbed by the job in hand will not only assist in you doing a better job, it will increase your chances of flow no matter what the task in hand. The flow state constantly prompts us to do better to enable the flow feelings to return. So push yourself to be better, chase a new task, skill, qualification, job, or hobby, and then keep chasing them for your whole life!

Read a book- Engross yourself in some other person's words and outlook. This will take your mind off yourself and give you a break.

Go get a cuddle – you'll be amazed how much a quick, friendly hug from somebody else will make you feel. No one around? No problem, give yourself a big hug. You deserve one!

Smile at yourself in the mirror – Of course we smile when we are happy, but did you know that good research points to the fact that we can smile ourselves happy? Pass on a smile to someone. It costs absolutely nothing and will raise their mood as well as yours.

You will be amazed at how a regular smile at yourself in the mirror uplifts you. Be proud of yourself. You are doing the very best job you can.

Have confidence – Pull your shoulders back, stand up straight, raise your arms a little and adopt a powerful stance. You are a unique mix of genes and you were born here for a reason. Fulfill your destiny, you have the ability to make things happen.

Plan your week – Make sure you plan some fun into your days and weeks, along with your workload. Try and include some exercise and socialising with friends. Putting things into your diary every week ensures you get your rest periods. Yes, we may and should work hard, but you must enjoy life too!

Exercise - No drug in the world can replace the benefits exercise gives us. Exercise is a statement to yourself that you are in charge of your body. This leads to a feeling of wellbeing that can stimulate your confidence and lead you to better control other events too. It really is such a great tonic and can help you to develop new friends.

Do the direct opposite – This is one of my favourites. So you may be anxious about something. Perhaps you are afraid to make a telephone call? Just do it. You may not want to go to the shops? Do it. You don't want to go the party? Do it. You don't want to go for a walk? Do it. You may not want to go to places you've never seen before? Do it. Traveling is a particularly good way to push your self. A new place and a new surrounding gives you lots of new perspectives.

This attitude gives you new horizons and will give you a new found confidence. I used to work in sales and one of the managers once told me that I ran the risk of becoming my own SPO (sales prevention officer). We think of reasons why we may not be able to make a sale instead of just trying. It's a similar concept. Just do it, try it, go there, meet them, buy it and stop creating your own barriers by doing the direct opposite.

Face your fears - Do your research until you know everything about your fear. This will assist you greatly in defeating it. Those who suppress their vulnerabilities are suppressing joy and life itself. By facing your fears YOU will have crossed a significant bridge, and will feel extremely proud of yourself. You've tried! Many never do. You've looked your fear straight between the eyes and tried to beat it. Well done indeed.

Eat more healthily – Our brains need nutrients, just like our bodies. A well-balanced diet includes protein from meat or fish, nuts, and seeds. You also need plenty of fruit and vegetables. A car won't work without the correct petrol and your body needs the correct nutrients, too. Please seriously consider this carefully, the ingredients to support your body and mind must be there. Nutrition is very important.

Sleep – You must try to maintain a good sleeping pattern. Keeping the light dim before you get to bed and avoiding computers and smart devices will help, as will the exercise you are hopefully doing. The daytime meditations and mindfulness that you will hopefully be practising will also help considerably. In mediation, you are training your brain to concentrate on nothing but your breathing. This is a great way to get to sleep too.

Buy some new clothes – Assuming you've got a bit of money to spare, getting yourself dressed up nicely can lift your mood and make you feel proud. This applies to men just as much as women.

I have a friend (who just happens to be a millionaire) who only shops in charity shops. Whenever I see him, he looks a million dollars. Even if you haven't got that much money to spare, there are some really low cost shops around to sparkle up your wardrobe.

Tidy up your living environment - Tidying your desk, your office, your flat, your room, your car, or your wardrobe, will give you a sense of order. Keep going once you've started and you'll be on a roll! Seeing these things tidy will reinforce to you that you are in a good place.

Get it off your chest – If you have a problem go tell a friend, relative, counselor or doctor. If you can't find somebody to talk to, speak to God, the universe, or anyone up there. Just getting things off your chest and letting the words flow in conversation often gives you some clarity, even if the recipient of the words says nothing. Hopefully this should give you a clearer view, and if not, at least you should get some relief by verbalising your issues. Sharing joy increases it: sharing pain lessens it.

Get it on paper – Take your thoughts out of your head and get them down on paper. This will significantly help you to work through it all methodically. Give yourself time. If it's a problem, get creative with possible answers. You will be amazed at how writing it down helps to clear your mind. Once the path forward is found, tear up the negative thoughts and sling them in the bin.

New thoughts can re-make you – YES, new thoughts can literally create a whole new world for you. Think optimistically and productively. These thoughts give you confidence, lift your spirit and put light into your life. A positive mind-set should hopefully lead to more happiness, and possibly a longer life, so embrace those new thoughts with real fervour.

Take time out to dream - With some careful planning you should be able to create some freedom in your life to achieve the things you want to do. Perhaps a less strenuous job may suit you, or even self-employment. Creating space can give you more time to plan, more time to think and more time to arrive in a happier place. Live your life honestly and not in a way that others expect of you. Follow your dreams; you only have one life to live.

Frame things well - How can I view this differently? Is there another perspective that I am missing? There are endless ways to view things. Find a viewpoint that you find reasonably acceptable. It doesn't have to be perfect, just good enough to allow you to move on productively. Things are not what they are, they are what we perceive them to be.

Distract yourself - If you launch yourself into a different task (particularly one that involves using your hands), it will give you time to clear your mind. I am a huge believer in doing something different to take my mind off a problem. My personal favourite distraction is a walk around the block. This is particularly helpful if I need to solve a problem. Just the act of walking seems to give me a clearer insight. I have seen good scientific research to support the increased clarity that a walk around the block can give you. (16)

Do something kind - Taking time out to help someone else is a great mood lifter. It could be as little as holding a door open for someone else, asking a neighbour if they want something from the local shop, making a cake for someone, taking out the trash, helping an old neighbour in their garden or clearing some snow in the winter. I'm sure you have lots of your own ideas.

Perhaps one of the nicest things you can do for someone is to show interest. We are all often wrapped up in our own lives. Taking a break from our own lives and allowing someone else to express themselves is a wonderful thing to do.

'There is nothing that makes you feel warmer at the base of your human soul, than being really kind to people'

Live in the moment and savour – Take time to smell the roses and be conscious of what is going on around you. Slow down and look carefully at what you are doing. You will be amazed at the little details you could be missing.

Take time to really enjoy each mouthful of food. Try taking twice as long to eat your food and savour each bite. Living in the moment we see more and miss less. Savour things, and you will get lots more enjoyment out of any event.

Simply abstaining or giving something up for a while drives our appreciation of it the next time we have it. In effect less is more, particularly when it comes to savouring. So don't worry if you are missing something, you are much more likely to enjoy and savour it the next time.

AS IF – Do you want to be happy, confident or strong? You will be amazed at how just behaving '**as if**' you already had these characteristics can create the state you wish for.

The power of suggestion is often all we need to take us right there. Believe you are confident and you will be.

The News - Approach the daily news and social media with caution. Maybe even stop listening to the news (or limiting it). You could be amazed at how this simple task could make you feel. Without the daily dose of negativity you can focus on all the good things around you. Try filtering it out of your life and focus on the present amazing things around you.

When it comes to social media ask yourself, "does it add or subtract from my happiness"? If it's not adding or uplifting you try limiting or stopping your exposure. Face-to-face relationships will always foster greater understanding and interest.

Choose friends wisely – Sometimes it's time to seek out new friends. I'm not saying dump your old friends, but just tweaking the time you spend with some of them may raise your spirits. Never ever believe that you are inferior to other people, you are not! May I suggest that positive, optimistic, upbeat and happy people will do you far more good.

Think Happy - Events can happen around us that sometimes we have absolutely no control over. These events can be exceptionally challenging, but how we respond to these events is completely in our control. Your brain obeys the instructions you give it. The good news is that we can form new neural networks and change the way we view things. Make a diary and list the high points of your day, then review them at night before bed. Happiness is a choice. Choose happiness.

Make positive affirmations - You might have an interview, a social occasion, or a task to do, but you may be a little nervous because you want to have a good time and succeed. Tell yourself how good you are with some positive self-affirmations. Blow yourself up, see your very best self and believe it!

"I can do this"

Think positively and optimistically, because good research shows it will possibly extend your life. (3)

Let it go - Harbouring any resentment or ill will to anyone could eventually eat into you if not controlled. You may have been mistreated, criticised or let down but please try to forgive. You needn't necessarily forget, but put it on the bottom shelf and don't go there. If we are not careful, by holding grievances we are holding back our own happiness. It's like locking yourself in jail.

Follow Pareto's 80/20 rule – It sounds a little silly but spend more time doing the things you enjoy. 80% of your results may come from 20% of your efforts, so take time out to know which these are. 20% of people may be bringing you 80% of happiness, so it makes sense to spend more time with them.

Take it easy - When we are stressed, hungry, tired, or ill, our thought processes can be hindered. You are more than likely to view things incorrectly and more likely to see a negative outcome based on your impeded ability to think clearly. Be easy on yourself, these thoughts will pass. It's just a rainy day, they always blow over, and the sun always shines again.

Problem Solve - "*I have not failed. I've just found 10,000 ways that won't work*" said prolific inventor Thomas Edison. You may not realise it but I guarantee that you have it within you to find another way forward. Try to distract yourself to help you answer your problem. Importantly, don't rush, give yourself some time to see clearly.

Avoid too much worry – Most of us have some negative self-chatter in our heads. It's helpful at low levels (it stops us doing silly things). Yet once we adopt a problem-solving attitude we are on the way to reducing our worries. Remember, it's not the event that occurs but our reaction to it that matters. Overthinking (or rumination) may be bad for us. We need to consider important things seriously, but if we are not careful, this can creep into everyday life and the result can be over analysing everything. Over thinking can be **'unhelpful'** much better to substitute it with a happiness raising activity or consider regular breaks using such techniques as mindfulness as described in the chapter 'The Wonderful anti-stress button'.

Change it – *"There is a certain relief in change, even though it may be from bad to worse. I have found when traveling in a stagecoach, that it is often a comfort to shift one's position and be bruised in a new place."*
Washington Irving who was born in 1783.

Sometimes things don't work out even after you've made a change but if you are prepared to accept that and take risks, you are definitely ready for a change.

Accept your mistakes – Don't let your pride get in the way. The more mistakes you make, the faster you will learn. Make 1000s of mistakes; live life to the full. Tomorrow is far more important than yesterday.

Be yourself – You have nothing to hide. You are beautiful just the way you are. Don't worry what others think, that's not your problem.

Don't make excuses – I accept that you may have a genuine reason for not progressing, but if it's money, time, others' opinions or your age holding you back, I disagree. Money can be saved. Time can be found if you're determined enough. Others' opinions can be dismissed. Finally, age? Well that's just a number!

Hold on – Experiencing the bad leads to the good. The most important lessons we learn are when things haven't gone our way. Be proud of yourself and, in time, you will be able to look back and see how strong, capable and resourceful you have become.

Busy yourself - The more variety you have in your life, the more interesting you will find it. Perhaps try something completely different. How do you know you won't like it until you've tried it?

Dare to Dream - Make time for yourself to achieve the things you'd like to do. Some goals and dreams will give you far more lasting happiness than others. For instance, a career you are completely dedicated to will give you great joy. Take some time out and have a think about the things that really matter to you. Being focused on achieving these things will fully engage you and leave you more fulfilled.

Three good things a day - Scientific research suggests that we can train ourselves to be happy by logging the daily things that uplift us. When you examine these, the change of focus creates a self-perpetuating, uplifting cycle. Begin your own notes or diary and jot down three good things every day.

Natural Happiness Hormones - This wonderful box of tricks can be released in many different ways. Oxytocin is known widely as the cuddle hormone. Go get a big hug or do something nice for someone, both have been shown to generate Oxytocin. Serotonin is generated when we exercise, eat carbohydrates or get in the sun. Endorphins are produced when we have a good laugh and this is great at reducing stress. Dopamine can kick in when we get a sense of achievement or when we listen to music.

Now I can see you - Being closely connected to others is one of the most wonderful things in the world. Knowing that someone accepts you (warts and all) should be treasured. Be true to yourself and it will enrich your life with the people that really matter.

Seek out laughter - It's great for stress relief. Oxygen floods into your lungs, your muscles contract, your blood pressure changes and your brain releases endorphins. WOW all this from just a good laugh. It is such a good mood changer and can give you a new perspective on problems. Sometimes the best thing to do is leave your problem at the door, go have a good laugh and come back with a new perspective.

I hope you've enjoyed the book. I've tried to bring you lots of ways to enable you to make a change, to raise your spirits and to bring a daily dose of happiness. I'm sure you will have guessed by now that it's my firmly held belief that irrespective of circumstances:

Happiness is a product of the goals and aims you set, your thoughts, and your purposely chosen attitude to life's events.

Your experience is only what you agree to, refuse to accept a script that is not of your design, be optimistic, have confidence in yourself and truly believe that:

YOU HAVE THE POWER TO CHANGE THINGS

I wholeheartedly believe in you...

Martin Hill is available for presentations and meetings to discuss his ideas further. He warmly welcomes presentations to schools, colleges and universities. He is also available for one-to-one confidential meetings with business directors and professionals. For further information please don't hesitate to email the following address.

martinhill@thehappinesssheme.com

SCIENCE BASED HAPPINESS

PART 5

THE '5 MINUTE' FOCUS

A DAILY JOURNEY TO POINT YOU
TO A HAPPIER PLACE

PLAN AND CREATE SOME ACTIONS

'The 5 Minute Focus' is the place you now engage the principles of the Happiness Scheme Book. The primary aim is to encourage the writing down (or journaling) of good, positive, optimistic thoughts and actions. This is YOUR 'action station' where you get to consider and plan your strategies. Research points to many things that can raise our happiness levels and framing events well (cognitive therapy) is a very helpful place to start.

Good mental health is being able to recognise your mood and to take action to raise it if required. Yet knowing something is absolutely 'useless' unless that knowledge is put into action.

DETERMINATION

Determination is key. It's up to you to decide how and when you start your path to more happiness, but given that this is probably one of the most important things you will do, getting organised will be extremely helpful.

To quote a passage by William Murray:

"Until one is committed there is the chance to draw back and subsequent ineffectiveness. But the moment one definitely commits oneself, then Providence moves too.

All sort of things occur to help that would never otherwise have occurred. A whole stream of events issues from the decision, raising in ones favour all manner of unforeseen incidents and assistance."

William Murray
(1951 The Scottish Himalayan Expedition)

THE SCIENCE
BEHIND
THE '5 MINUTE' FOCUS

Please do not underestimate the power behind this section. Its core is based on scientific principles and the reference links are at the back of the book. The following are the principal activities, which science indicates as ways to raise your mood.

The influence of self-talk and mental imagery (1)
The benefits of mindfulness (6)
The benefits of appreciation and gratitude (9)
Kindness and Happiness (10)
Smiling (11)
Savouring (12)
Exercise and the benefits to your mood (20)

Theses daily actions have been proven beneficial to your health happiness and well being.

This really is
Science Based Happiness!

PLEASE REMEMBER, **YOU WERE BORN FOR A REASON** AND YOU **ALWAYS** HAVE THE POWER TO **CHANGE** THINGS.

START YOUR FOCUS

Simply fill out the journal at night and have a quick read in the morning too. This is a guided plan to hopefully take you to a happier place. The structure is geared to a 5-day working week, with 2 relatively free weekend days (please adjust this to your personal schedule if you work weekends).

We start with goals and dreams on the first page, assuming a Sunday, but any days are fine to start. Fill in your desired dreams and what you can do to get there, picturing 'your best possible self' achieving your goal. To begin with though you ideally need to fill out your daily affirmations, as these will help you get to where you want to be.

You are more likely to do things that you enjoy. If something isn't floating your boat anymore, don't fret. Try something else or do it in a different way to keep things fresh. We are all different when it comes to finding things we enjoy, for instance the smiling in the mirror task is listed once a week but there's nothing stopping you doing this every day if you enjoy it.

It's helpful to 'fully commit' to filling in your 5 Minute Focus, but don't beat yourself up if you happen to miss a day or two, just get back on track at your first opportunity. We are all different but Phillipa Lally and her colleagues from University College London suggest that it takes on average 66 days to form a habit so we've included 77 pages in The 5 minute Focus. That said you should see improvements in your mood very quickly, it's just a question of holding on to these methods and making them habitual.

May I wish you all the best I have a wholehearted belief in you.

BRING YOUR 'BEST POSSIBLE SELF' TO THE FRONT

YOU 'CAN' DO THIS !

SELF-AFFIRMATIONS

"We are what we repeatedly do. Excellence then is not an act, but a habit." ARISTOTLE

We build up feelings of security or insecurity by how we think. The power of thought is exceptionally influential on our feelings and emotions. What we are simply doing here is training your brain to go in the direction YOU have chosen it to go in, rather than let it wander where it likes.

See the chapter beginning on Page 37 on how to construct these. Ideally you need to repeat these three times per day with real passion and good imagination so make sure you put them in an easily accessible place, the fridge, the bathroom perhaps your mobile device? Tweak them, stay with the same ones or create some new ones, it's your choice. You can create as many as you wish ☺☺!

My self-affirmations for next month are:

_____

_____

_____

_____

_____

_____

_____

_____

_____

_____

Begin your daily 5 minute focus, BEST of luck!

Day   Date   (Maybe Sunday?) The 5 Minute Focus

Quote...

"If we can dream something, if we can picture something, we can make it a reality"
Jonah Lomu

GOALS AND DREAMS (Page 109)
What goals and dreams can I imagine?

_____
_____
_____

WHAT STEPS DO I NEED TO TAKE TO GET THERE (Page 40)
Imagine and picture your 'BEST POSSIBLE SELF'

_____
_____
_____

PRODUCTIVE THINGS (Page 108)
What are the 5 most productive things I can do tomorrow?

1 _____
2 _____
3 _____
4 _____
5 _____

PRESS THE ANTI-STRESS BUTTON (Page 50)
When will I take my 3 x 2 minute breaks tomorrow?

1) _____   2) _____   3) _____

GET OFF YOUR BOTTOM (Page 99)
No drug can replace the benefits of exercise. So tomorrow I'm going to:

_____

GRATEFULL THINGS (Page 94)
What are the 3 things I am most grateful for today?

1 _____
2 _____
3 _____

Day   Date   The 5 Minute Focus

Quote...

"Once we anticipate a specific outcome will occur, our subsequent thoughts and behaviours will actually help to bring that outcome to fruition". **Garry, Michael, Kirsch (Havard Medical School and Plymouth University)**

PRODUCTIVE THINGS (Page 108)
What are the 5 most productive things I can do tomorrow?

1 _____
2 _____
3 _____
4 _____
5 _____

DAILY AFFIRMATIONS (Page 37)
I am doing my self-affirmations tomorrow at the following times.

1) _____ 2) _____ 3) _____

SAVOURING (Page 130)
Slow down, live in the moment. Tomorrow I look forward to savouring, these 3 things.

1 _____
2 _____
3 _____

PRESS THE ANTI-STRESS BUTTON (Page 50)
When will I take my 3 x 2 minute breaks tomorrow?

1) _____ 2) _____ 3) _____

GET OFF YOUR BOTTOM (Page 99)
No drug can replace the benefits of exercise. So tomorrow I'm going to:

_____

GRATEFULL THINGS (Page 94)
What are the 3 things I am most grateful for today?

1 _____
2 _____
3 _____

Day   Date   The 5 Minute Focus

Quote...

"Do not spoil what you have by desiring what you have not; remember that what you now have was once among the things you only hoped for." Epicurus

PRODUCTIVE THINGS (Page 108)
What are the 5 most productive things I can do tomorrow?

1 _____
2 _____
3 _____
4 _____
5 _____

DAILY AFFIRMATIONS (Page 37)
I am doing my self-affirmations tomorrow at the following times.

1) _____ 2) _____ 3) _____

KARMA (Page 44)
'What goes around comes around'
My small favour for someone else today is:

_____

PRESS THE ANTI-STRESS BUTTON (Page 50)
When will I take my 3 x 2 minute breaks tomorrow?

1) _____ 2) _____ 3) _____

GET OFF YOUR BOTTOM (Page 99)
No drug can replace the benefits of exercise. So tomorrow I'm going to:

_____

GRATEFULL THINGS (Page 94)
What are the 3 things I am most grateful for today?

1 _____
2 _____
3 _____

Day   Date   The 5 Minute Focus

Quote...

"Everything you can imagine is real."
Pablo Picasso

PRODUCTIVE THINGS (Page 108)
What are the 5 most productive things I can do tomorrow?

1 _____
2 _____
3 _____
4 _____
5 _____

DAILY AFFIRMATIONS (Page 37)
I am doing my self-affirmations tomorrow at the following times.

1) _____ 2) _____ 3) _____

'SMILE' (Page 125)
Smile at yourself in the mirror, and be proud, you've done your best!
I'm smiling at my self tomorrow 3 times at the following times:

1) _____ 2) _____ 3) _____

PRESS THE ANTI-STRESS BUTTON (Page 50)
When will I take my 3 x 2 minute breaks tomorrow?

1) _____ 2) _____ 3) _____

GET OFF YOUR BOTTOM (Page 99)
No drug can replace the benefits of exercise. So tomorrow I'm going to:

_____

GRATEFULL THINGS (Page 94)
What are the 3 things I am most grateful for today?

1 _____
2 _____
3 _____

Day   Date   The 5 Minute Focus

Quote...

"Sometimes it doesn't matter if the glass is half empty or half full. It's just good to be grateful that you have a glass and there is something in it." Anon

PRODUCTIVE THINGS (Page 108)
What are the 5 most productive things I can do tomorrow?

1 _____
2 _____
3 _____
4 _____
5 _____

DAILY AFFIRMATIONS (Page 37)
I am doing my self-affirmations tomorrow at the following times.

1) _____ 2) _____ 3) _____

HAPPINESS 'REFRAME' (Page 86)
If anything pops into my head to annoy me I will simply deal with it, let it go, or think about it from a new perspective. My new perspective tomorrow is:

_____

PRESS THE ANTI-STRESS BUTTON (Page 50)
When will I take my 3 x 2 minute breaks tomorrow?

1) _____ 2) _____ 3) _____

GET OFF YOUR BOTTOM (Page 99)
No drug can replace the benefits of exercise. So tomorrow I'm going to:

_____

GRATEFULL THINGS (Page 94)
What are the 3 things I am most grateful for today?

1 _____
2 _____
3 _____

Day   Date   The 5 Minute Focus

Quote...

"Finish each day and be done with it. You have done what you could." **Ralph Waldo Emerson**

GET IN THE FLOW THIS WEEKEND (Page 127)

Try your own ideas, were all so different (or a few of the following) Listen to music. Visit a really good friend. Read a book. Cook something new. Get a cuddle. Plan your dreams. Plan your week ensuring you do things you enjoy. Tidy your environment. Try a new task or hobby. Go somewhere different. Seek out some laughter (even on the tele) or in good company. Engage in a new hobby or sport. Gardening, yes this actually appeals to some. Golf, tennis, a walk or your favourite hobby, in fact ANYTHING you gain pleasure from.

My FLOW task this weekend is

DAILY AFFIRMATIONS (Page 37)
I am doing my self-affirmations tomorrow at the following times.

1)_____ 2)_____ 3) _____

"AS IF" (Page 35)
Blow yourself up a bit and believe it, you can hold any state you want. Just colourfully visualise the state you wish for and make it happen in reality. Today I behave as if ...

DON'T OVERTHINK BE HAPPY (Page 90)
Stop overthinking and ruminating trust it will all turn out OK.
I'm thinking optimistically tomorrow about:

GET OFF YOUR BOTTOM (Page 99)
No drug can replace the benefits of exercise. So tomorrow I'm going to:

GRATEFULL THINGS (Page 94)
What are the 3 things I am most grateful for today?

1 _____
2 _____
3 _____

Day   Date   The 5 Minute Focus

Quote...

"Hunger and ability are the seeds of success, the good news is you can develop both." Martin Hill

KINDNESS (Page 96)
I will spread some kindness tomorrow by doing these 5 things; of course you can spread these through the week if you wish.

1. _____
2. _____
3. _____
4. _____
5. _____

SAVOURING (Page 130)
Slow down, live in the moment. Tomorrow I look forward to savouring:

_____

THREE GOOD THINGS (Page 115)
What 3 good things happened today?

1. _____
2. _____
3. _____

PRESS THE ANTI-STRESS BUTTON (Page 50)
When will I take my 3 x 2 minute breaks tomorrow?

1) _____ 2) _____ 3) _____

GET OFF YOUR BOTTOM (Page 99)
No drug can replace the benefits of exercise. So tomorrow I'm going to:

_____

GRATEFULL THINGS (Page 94)
What are the 3 things I am most grateful for today?

1. _____
2. _____
3. _____

Day   Date   (Maybe Sunday?) The 5 Minute Focus

Quote...

"My interest is in the future because I am going to spend the rest of my life there" **Charles Kettering**

GOALS AND DREAMS (Page 109)
What goals and dreams can I imagine?

_____

_____

_____

WHAT STEPS DO I NEED TO TAKE TO GET THERE (Page 40)
Imagine and picture your 'BEST POSSIBLE SELF'

_____

_____

PRODUCTIVE THINGS (Page 108)
What are the 5 most productive things I can do tomorrow?

1 _____
2 _____
3 _____
4 _____
5 _____

PRESS THE ANTI-STRESS BUTTON (Page 50)
When will I take my 3 x 2 minute breaks tomorrow?

1) _____ 2) _____ 3) _____

GET OFF YOUR BOTTOM (Page 99)
No drug can replace the benefits of exercise. So tomorrow I'm going to:

_____

GRATEFULL THINGS (Page 94)
What are the 3 things I am most grateful for today?

1 _____
2 _____
3 _____

Day   Date   The 5 Minute Focus

Quote...

"We are what we repeatedly do. Excellence then is not an act, but a habit." Aristotle

PRODUCTIVE THINGS (Page 108)
What are the 5 most productive things I can do tomorrow?

1 _____
2 _____
3 _____
4 _____
5 _____

DAILY AFFIRMATIONS (Page 37)
I am doing my self-affirmations tomorrow at the following times.

1) _____ 2) _____ 3) _____

SAVOURING (Page 130)
Slow down, live in the moment. Tomorrow I look forward to savouring, these 3 things.

1 _____
2 _____
3 _____

PRESS THE ANTI-STRESS BUTTON (Page 50)
When will I take my 3 x 2 minute breaks tomorrow?

1) _____ 2) _____ 3) _____

GET OFF YOUR BOTTOM (Page 99)
No drug can replace the benefits of exercise. So tomorrow I'm going to:

_____

GRATEFULL THINGS (Page 94)
What are the 3 things I am most grateful for today?

1 _____
2 _____
3 _____

Day   Date   The 5 Minute Focus

Quote...

"If you're going through hell - keep going."
Winston Churchill

PRODUCTIVE THINGS (Page 108)
What are the 5 most productive things I can do tomorrow?

1 _____
2 _____
3 _____
4 _____
5 _____

DAILY AFFIRMATIONS (Page 37)
I am doing my self-affirmations tomorrow at the following times.

1)_____ 2)_____ 3) _____

KARMA (Page 44)
'What goes around comes around'
My small favour for someone else today is:

PRESS THE ANTI-STRESS BUTTON (Page 50)
When will I take my 3 x 2 minute breaks tomorrow?

1)_____ 2)_____ 3) _____

GET OFF YOUR BOTTOM (Page 99)
No drug can replace the benefits of exercise. So tomorrow I'm going to:

GRATEFULL THINGS (Page 94)
What are the 3 things I am most grateful for today?

1 _____
2 _____
3 _____

Day   Date   The 5 Minute Focus

Quote...

"A jug fills drop by drop."
Buddha

PRODUCTIVE THINGS (Page 108)
What are the 5 most productive things I can do tomorrow?

1 _____
2 _____
3 _____
4 _____
5 _____

DAILY AFFIRMATIONS (Page 37)
I am doing my self-affirmations tomorrow at the following times.

1) _____ 2) _____ 3) _____

'SMILE' (Page 125)
Smile at yourself in the mirror, and be proud, you've done your best!
I'm smiling at my self tomorrow 3 times at the following times:

1) _____ 2) _____ 3) _____

PRESS THE ANTI-STRESS BUTTON (Page 50)
When will I take my 3 x 2 minute breaks tomorrow?

1) _____ 2) _____ 3) _____

GET OFF YOUR BOTTOM (Page 99)
No drug can replace the benefits of exercise. So tomorrow I'm going to:

_____

GRATEFULL THINGS (Page 94)
What are the 3 things I am most grateful for today?

1 _____
2 _____
3 _____

Day   Date   The 5 Minute Focus

Quote...

"We first then make our habits, then our habits make us"
John Dryden

PRODUCTIVE THINGS (Page 108)
What are the 5 most productive things I can do tomorrow?

1 _____
2 _____
3 _____
4 _____
5 _____

DAILY AFFIRMATIONS (Page 37)
I am doing my self-affirmations tomorrow at the following times.
1) _____ 2) _____ 3) _____

HAPPINESS 'REFRAME' (Page 86)
If anything pops into my head to annoy me I will simply deal with it, let it go, or think about it from a new perspective. My new perspective tomorrow is:

_____

PRESS THE ANTI-STRESS BUTTON (Page 50)
When will I take my 3 x 2 minute breaks tomorrow?

1) _____ 2) _____ 3) _____

GET OFF YOUR BOTTOM (Page 99)
No drug can replace the benefits of exercise. So tomorrow I'm going to:

_____

GRATEFULL THINGS (Page 94)
What are the 3 things I am most grateful for today?

1 _____
2 _____
3 _____

Day   Date   The 5 Minute Focus

Quote...
"The best way to cheer yourself up is to try to cheer somebody else up" **Mark Twain**

GET IN THE FLOW THIS WEEKEND (Page 127)

Try your own ideas, were all so different (or a few of the following) Listen to music. Visit a really good friend. Read a book. Cook something new. Get a cuddle. Plan your dreams. Plan your week ensuring you do things you enjoy. Tidy your environment. Try a new task or hobby. Go somewhere different. Seek out some laughter (even on the tele) or in good company. Engage in a new hobby or sport. Gardening, yes this actually appeals to some. Golf, tennis, a walk or your favourite hobby, in fact ANYTHING you gain pleasure from.
My FLOW task this weekend is

DAILY AFFIRMATIONS (Page 37)
I am doing my self-affirmations tomorrow at the following times.
1) _____ 2) _____ 3) _____

"AS IF" (Page 35)
Blow yourself up a bit and believe it, you can hold any state you want. Just colourfully visualise the state you wish for and make it happen in reality. Today I will behave as if...

DON'T OVERTHINK BE HAPPY (Page 90)
Stop overthinking and ruminating trust it will all turn out OK.
I'm thinking optimistically tomorrow about:

GET OFF YOUR BOTTOM (Page 99)
No drug can replace the benefits of exercise. So tomorrow I'm going to:

GRATEFULL THINGS (Page 94)
What are the 3 things I am most grateful for today?

1 _____
2 _____
3 _____

Day   Date   The 5 Minute Focus

Quote...

"I never hit a shot, not even in practice, without having a very sharp in-focus picture of it in my head." Jack Nicklaus

KINDNESS (Page 96)
I will spread some kindness tomorrow by doing these 5 things; of course you can spread these through the week if you wish.

1 _____
2 _____
3 _____
4 _____
5 _____

SAVOURING (Page 130)
Slow down, live in the moment. Tomorrow I look forward to savouring:

_____

THREE GOOD THINGS (Page 115)
What 3 good things happened today?

1 _____
2 _____
3 _____

PRESS THE ANTI-STRESS BUTTON (Page 50)
When will I take my 3 x 2 minute breaks tomorrow?

1) _____ 2) _____ 3) _____

GET OFF YOUR BOTTOM (Page 99)
No drug can replace the benefits of exercise. So tomorrow I'm going to:

_____

GRATEFULL THINGS (Page 94)
What are the 3 things I am most grateful for today?

1 _____
2 _____
3 _____

Day   Date   (Maybe Sunday?)   The 5 Minute Focus

Quote...

"As we look ahead into the next century, leaders will be those who empower others." **Bill Gates**

GOALS AND DREAMS (Page 109)
What goals and dreams can I imagine?

_____
_____
_____

WHAT STEPS DO I NEED TO TAKE TO GET THERE (Page 40)
Imagine and picture your 'BEST POSSIBLE SELF'

_____
_____
_____

PRODUCTIVE THINGS (Page 108)
What are the 5 most productive things I can do tomorrow?

1 _____
2 _____
3 _____
4 _____
5 _____

PRESS THE ANTI-STRESS BUTTON (Page 50)
When will I take my 3 x 2 minute breaks tomorrow?

1) _____   2) _____   3) _____

GET OFF YOUR BOTTOM (Page 99)
No drug can replace the benefits of exercise. So tomorrow I'm going to:

_____

GRATEFULL THINGS (Page 94)
What are the 3 things I am most grateful for today?

1 _____
2 _____
3 _____

Day   Date   The 5 Minute Focus

Quote...

"The best way to predict the future is to engineer it." **MartinHill**

PRODUCTIVE THINGS (Page 108)
What are the 5 most productive things I can do tomorrow?

1 _____
2 _____
3 _____
4 _____
5 _____

DAILY AFFIRMATIONS (Page 37)
I am doing my self-affirmations tomorrow at the following times.

1) _____ 2) _____ 3) _____

SAVOURING (Page 130)
Slow down, live in the moment. Tomorrow I look forward to savouring, these 3 things.

1 _____
2 _____
3 _____

PRESS THE ANTI-STRESS BUTTON (Page 50)
When will I take my 3 x 2 minute breaks tomorrow?

1) _____ 2) _____ 3) _____

GET OFF YOUR BOTTOM (Page 99)
No drug can replace the benefits of exercise. So tomorrow I'm going to:

_____

GRATEFULL THINGS (Page 94)
What are the 3 things I am most grateful for today?

1 _____
2 _____
3 _____

Day   Date   The 5 Minute Focus

Quote...

"Everything is practice."
Pele (one of the best footballers ever born)

PRODUCTIVE THINGS (Page 108)
What are the 5 most productive things I can do tomorrow?

1 _____
2 _____
3 _____
4 _____
5 _____

DAILY AFFIRMATIONS (Page 37)
I am doing my self-affirmations tomorrow at the following times.

1) _____   2) _____   3) _____

KARMA (Page 44)
'What goes around comes around'
My small favour for someone else today is:

_____

PRESS THE ANTI-STRESS BUTTON (Page 50)
When will I take my 3 x 2 minute breaks tomorrow?

1) _____   2) _____   3) _____

GET OFF YOUR BOTTOM (Page 99)
No drug can replace the benefits of exercise. So tomorrow I'm going to:

_____

GRATEFULL THINGS (Page 94)
What are the 3 things I am most grateful for today?

1 _____
2 _____
3 _____

Day   Date   The 5 Minute Focus

Quote...

"I am always doing things I can't do – that's how I get to do them." **Pablo Picasso**

PRODUCTIVE THINGS (Page 108)
What are the 5 most productive things I can do tomorrow?

1 _____
2 _____
3 _____
4 _____
5 _____

DAILY AFFIRMATIONS (Page 37)
I am doing my self-affirmations tomorrow at the following times.

1) _____ 2) _____ 3) _____

'SMILE' (Page 125)
Smile at yourself in the mirror, and be proud, you've done your best! I'm smiling at my self tomorrow 3 times at the following times:

1) _____ 2) _____ 3) _____

PRESS THE ANTI-STRESS BUTTON (Page 50)
When will I take my 3 x 2 minute breaks tomorrow?

1) _____ 2) _____ 3) _____

GET OFF YOUR BOTTOM (Page 99)
No drug can replace the benefits of exercise. So tomorrow I'm going to:

_____

GRATEFULL THINGS (Page 94)
What are the 3 things I am most grateful for today?

1 _____
2 _____
3 _____

Day   Date   The 5 Minute Focus

Quote...

"Things turn out best for people who make the best of the way things turn out" John Wooden

PRODUCTIVE THINGS (Page 108)
What are the 5 most productive things I can do tomorrow?

1 _____
2 _____
3 _____
4 _____
5 _____

DAILY AFFIRMATIONS (Page 37)
I am doing my self-affirmations tomorrow at the following times.

1) _____ 2) _____ 3) _____

HAPPINESS 'REFRAME' (Page 86)
If anything pops into my head to annoy me I will simply deal with it, let it go, or think about it from a new perspective. My new perspective tomorrow is:

_____

PRESS THE ANTI-STRESS BUTTON (Page 50)
When will I take my 3 x 2 minute breaks tomorrow?

1) _____ 2) _____ 3) _____

GET OFF YOUR BOTTOM (Page 99)
No drug can replace the benefits of exercise. So tomorrow I'm going to:

_____

GRATEFULL THINGS (Page 94)
What are the 3 things I am most grateful for today?

1 _____
2 _____
3 _____

Day   Date   The 5 Minute Focus

Quote...

"I am the best in the world this is what I tell myself"
Cristiano Ronaldo

GET IN THE FLOW THIS WEEKEND (Page 127)

Try your own ideas, were all so different (or a few of the following) Listen to music. Visit a really good friend. Read a book. Cook something new. Get a cuddle. Plan your dreams. Plan your week ensuring you do things you enjoy. Tidy your environment. Try a new task or hobby. Go somewhere different. Seek out some laughter (even on the tele) or in good company. Engage in a new hobby or sport. Gardening, yes this actually appeals to some. Golf, tennis, a walk or your favourite hobby, in fact anything you gain pleasure from. My FLOW task this weekend is

___

DAILY AFFIRMATIONS (Page 37)

I am doing my self-affirmations tomorrow at the following times.

1)_____ 2)_____ 3) _____

"AS IF" (Page 35)

Blow yourself up a bit and believe it, you can hold any state you want. Just colourfully visualise the state you wish for and make it happen in reality. Today I will behave as if...

___

DON'T OVERTHINK BE HAPPY (Page 90)

Stop overthinking and ruminating trust it will all turn out OK.
I'm thinking optimistically tomorrow about:

___

GET OFF YOUR BOTTOM (Page 99)

No drug can replace the benefits of exercise. So tomorrow I'm going to:

___

GRATEFULL THINGS (Page 94)

What are the 3 things I am most grateful for today?

1 _____
2 _____
3 _____

Day   Date   The 5 Minute Focus

Quote...

"It's lack of faith that makes people afraid of meeting challenges, and I believe in myself." **Muhammad Ali**

KINDNESS (Page 96)
I will spread some kindness tomorrow by doing these 5 things; of course you can spread these through the week if you wish.

1. _____
2. _____
3. _____
4. _____
5. _____

SAVOURING (Page 130)
Slow down, live in the moment. Tomorrow I look forward to savouring:

_____

THREE GOOD THINGS (Page 115)
What 3 good things happened today?

1. _____
2. _____
3. _____

PRESS THE ANTI-STRESS BUTTON (Page 50)
When will I take my 3 x 2 minute breaks tomorrow?

1) _____   2) _____   3) _____

GET OFF YOUR BOTTOM (Page 99)
No drug can replace the benefits of exercise. So tomorrow I'm going to:

_____

GRATEFULL THINGS (Page 94)
What are the 3 things I am most grateful for today?

1. _____
2. _____
3. _____

Day   Date   (Maybe Sunday?) The 5 Minute Focus

Quote...

"Man is a goal-seeking animal. His life only has meaning if he is reaching out and striving for his goals." Aristotle

GOALS AND DREAMS (Page 109)
What goals and dreams can I imagine?

_____
_____
_____
_____

WHAT STEPS DO I NEED TO TAKE TO GET THERE (Page 40)
Imagine and picture your 'BEST POSSIBLE SELF'

_____
_____
_____
_____

PRODUCTIVE THINGS (Page 108)
What are the 5 most productive things I can do tomorrow?

1 _____
2 _____
3 _____
4 _____
5 _____

PRESS THE ANTI-STRESS BUTTON (Page 50)
When will I take my 3 x 2 minute breaks tomorrow?

1) _____ 2) _____ 3) _____

GET OFF YOUR BOTTOM (Page 99)
No drug can replace the benefits of exercise. So tomorrow I'm going to:

_____
_____

GRATEFULL THINGS (Page 94)
What are the 3 things I am most grateful for today?

1 _____
2 _____
3 _____

Day   Date   The 5 Minute Focus

Quote...

"Nothing is particularly hard if you divide it in to small jobs." **Henry Ford**

PRODUCTIVE THINGS (Page 108)
What are the 5 most productive things I can do tomorrow?

1 _____
2 _____
3 _____
4 _____
5 _____

DAILY AFFIRMATIONS (Page 37)
I am doing my self-affirmations tomorrow at the following times.

1) _____ 2) _____ 3) _____

SAVOURING (Page 130)
Slow down, live in the moment. Tomorrow I look forward to savouring, these 3 things.

1 _____
2 _____
3 _____

PRESS THE ANTI-STRESS BUTTON (Page 50)
When will I take my 3 x 2 minute breaks tomorrow?

1) _____ 2) _____ 3) _____

GET OFF YOUR BOTTOM (Page 99)
No drug can replace the benefits of exercise. So tomorrow I'm going to:

_____

GRATEFULL THINGS (Page 94)
What are the 3 things I am most grateful for today?

1 _____
2 _____
3 _____

Day   Date   The 5 Minute Focus

Quote...

"I always prefer to believe the best of everybody, it saves so much trouble" **Rudyard Kipling**

PRODUCTIVE THINGS (Page 108)
What are the 5 most productive things I can do tomorrow?

1 _____
2 _____
3 _____
4 _____
5 _____

DAILY AFFIRMATIONS (Page 37)
I am doing my self-affirmations tomorrow at the following times.

1) _____ 2) _____ 3) _____

KARMA (Page 44)
'What goes around comes around'
My small favour for someone else today is:

_____

PRESS THE ANTI-STRESS BUTTON (Page 50)
When will I take my 3 x 2 minute breaks tomorrow?

1) _____ 2) _____ 3) _____

GET OFF YOUR BOTTOM (Page 99)
No drug can replace the benefits of exercise. So tomorrow I'm going to:

_____

GRATEFULL THINGS (Page 94)
What are the 3 things I am most grateful for today?

1 _____
2 _____
3 _____

Day   Date   The 5 Minute Focus

Quote...

"Let me tell you the secret that has led me to my goal – my strength lies solely in my tenacity." **Louis Pasteur**

PRODUCTIVE THINGS (Page 108)
What are the 5 most productive things I can do tomorrow?

1 _____
2 _____
3 _____
4 _____
5 _____

DAILY AFFIRMATIONS (Page 37)
I am doing my self-affirmations tomorrow at the following times.

1) _____   2) _____   3) _____

'SMILE' (Page 125)
Smile at yourself in the mirror, and be proud, you've done your best!
I'm smiling at my self tomorrow 3 times at the following times:

1) _____   2) _____   3) _____

PRESS THE ANTI-STRESS BUTTON (Page 50)
When will I take my 3 x 2 minute breaks tomorrow?

1) _____   2) _____   3) _____

GET OFF YOUR BOTTOM (Page 99)
No drug can replace the benefits of exercise. So tomorrow I'm going to:

GRATEFULL THINGS (Page 94)
What are the 3 things I am most grateful for today?

1 _____
2 _____
3 _____

Day   Date   The 5 Minute Focus

Quote...
"The will to win, the desire to succeed, the urge to reach your full potential... these are the keys that will unlock the door to personal excellence." **Confucius**

PRODUCTIVE THINGS (Page 108)
What are the 5 most productive things I can do tomorrow?

1. _____
2. _____
3. _____
4. _____
5. _____

DAILY AFFIRMATIONS (Page 37)
I am doing my self-affirmations tomorrow at the following times.

1) _____ 2) _____ 3) _____

HAPPINESS 'REFRAME' (Page 86)
If anything pops into my head to annoy me I will simply deal with it, let it go, or think about it from a new perspective. My new perspective tomorrow is:

_____

PRESS THE ANTI-STRESS BUTTON (Page 50)
When will I take my 3 x 2 minute breaks tomorrow?

1) _____ 2) _____ 3) _____

GET OFF YOUR BOTTOM (Page 99)
No drug can replace the benefits of exercise. So tomorrow I'm going to:

_____

GRATEFULL THINGS (Page 94)
What are the 3 things I am most grateful for today?

1. _____
2. _____
3. _____

Day   Date   The 5 Minute Focus

Quote...

"If you can dream it, you can do it."
Walt Disney

GET IN THE FLOW THIS WEEKEND (Page 127)

Try your own ideas, were all so different (or a few of the following) Listen to music. Visit a really good friend. Read a book. Cook something new. Get a cuddle. Plan your dreams. Plan your week ensuring you do things you enjoy. Tidy your environment. Try a new task or hobby. Go somewhere different. Seek out some laughter (even on the tele) or in good company. Engage in a new hobby or sport. Gardening, yes this actually appeals to some. Golf, tennis, a walk or your favourite hobby, in fact anything you gain pleasure from. My FLOW task this weekend is

---

DAILY AFFIRMATIONS (Page 37)
I am doing my self-affirmations tomorrow at the following times.
1)_____ 2)_____ 3) _____

"AS IF" (Page 35)
Blow yourself up a bit and believe it, you can hold any state you want. Just colourfully visualise the state you wish for and make it happen in reality. Today I will behave as if...

DON'T OVERTHINK BE HAPPY (Page 90)
Stop overthinking and ruminating trust it will all turn out OK.
I'm thinking optimistically tomorrow about:

GET OFF YOUR BOTTOM (Page 99)
No drug can replace the benefits of exercise. So tomorrow I'm going to:

GRATEFULL THINGS (Page 94)
What are the 3 things I am most grateful for today?

1 _____
2 _____
3 _____

Day   Date   The 5 Minute Focus

Quote...

"You are never too old to set another goal or to dream a new dream." **C. S. Lewis**

KINDNESS (Page 96)
I will spread some kindness tomorrow by doing these 5 things; of course you can spread these through the week if you wish.

1. _____
2. _____
3. _____
4. _____
5. _____

SAVOURING (Page 130)
Slow down, live in the moment. Tomorrow I look forward to savouring:

_____

THREE GOOD THINGS (Page 115)
What 3 good things happened today?

1. _____
2. _____
3. _____

PRESS THE ANTI-STRESS BUTTON (Page 50)
When will I take my 3 x 2 minute breaks tomorrow?

1) _____ 2) _____ 3) _____

GET OFF YOUR BOTTOM (Page 99)
No drug can replace the benefits of exercise. So tomorrow I'm going to:

_____

GRATEFULL THINGS (Page 94)
What are the 3 things I am most grateful for today?

1. _____
2. _____
3. _____

Day   Date   (Maybe Sunday?) The 5 Minute Focus

Quote...
   "By failing to prepare, you are preparing to fail."
   Benjamin Franklin

GOALS AND DREAMS (Page 109)
What goals and dreams can I imagine?

_____
_____
_____

WHAT STEPS DO I NEED TO TAKE TO GET THERE (Page 40)
Imagine and picture your 'BEST POSSIBLE SELF'

_____
_____
_____

PRODUCTIVE THINGS (Page 108)
What are the 5 most productive things I can do tomorrow?

1 _____
2 _____
3 _____
4 _____
5 _____

PRESS THE ANTI-STRESS BUTTON (Page 50)
When will I take my 3 x 2 minute breaks tomorrow?

1) _____   2) _____   3) _____

GET OFF YOUR BOTTOM (Page 99)
No drug can replace the benefits of exercise. So tomorrow I'm going to:

_____

GRATEFULL THINGS (Page 94)
What are the 3 things I am most grateful for today?

1 _____
2 _____
3 _____

SELF-AFFIRMATIONS
YOUR CHANCE FOR A REVIEW, ANY ADJUSTMENTS NEEDED OR ALL COOL? ☺☺

We build up feelings of security or insecurity by how we think. The power of thought is exceptionally influential on our feelings and emotions. What we are simply doing here is training your brain to go in the direction YOU have chosen it to go in, rather than let it wander where it likes. See the chapter beginning on Page 37 on how to construct these.

My self-affirmations for next month are:

_____
_____
_____
_____
_____
_____
_____
_____
_____
_____
_____
_____
_____
_____
_____
_____
_____
_____

Day   Date   The 5 Minute Focus

Quote...

"The difference between the impossible and the possible lies in a man's determination" Tommy Lasorda

PRODUCTIVE THINGS (Page 108)
What are the 5 most productive things I can do tomorrow?

1 _____
2 _____
3 _____
4 _____
5 _____

DAILY AFFIRMATIONS (Page 37)
I am doing my self-affirmations tomorrow at the following times.

1) _____ 2) _____ 3) _____

SAVOURING (Page 130)
Slow down, live in the moment. Tomorrow I look forward to savouring, these 3 things.

1 _____
2 _____
3 _____

PRESS THE ANTI-STRESS BUTTON (Page 50)
When will I take my 3 x 2 minute breaks tomorrow?

1) _____ 2) _____ 3) _____

GET OFF YOUR BOTTOM (Page 99)
No drug can replace the benefits of exercise. So tomorrow I'm going to:

_____

GRATEFULL THINGS (Page 94)
What are the 3 things I am most grateful for today?

1 _____
2 _____
3 _____

Day   Date   The 5 Minute Focus

Quote...
"Either you run the day or the day runs you"
Jim Rohn

PRODUCTIVE THINGS (Page 108)
What are the 5 most productive things I can do tomorrow?

1 _____
2 _____
3 _____
4 _____
5 _____

DAILY AFFIRMATIONS (Page 37)
I am doing my self-affirmations tomorrow at the following times.

1) _____ 2) _____ 3) _____

KARMA (Page 44)
'What goes around comes around'
My small favour for someone else today is:

_____

PRESS THE ANTI-STRESS BUTTON (Page 50)
When will I take my 3 x 2 minute breaks tomorrow?

1) _____ 2) _____ 3) _____

GET OFF YOUR BOTTOM (Page 99)
No drug can replace the benefits of exercise. So tomorrow I'm going to:

_____

GRATEFULL THINGS (Page 94)
What are the 3 things I am most grateful for today?

1 _____
2 _____
3 _____

Day   Date   The 5 Minute Focus

Quote...

There is no passion to be found playing small - in settling for a life that is less than the one you are capable of living.
Nelson Mandela

PRODUCTIVE THINGS (Page 108)
What are the 5 most productive things I can do tomorrow?

1 _____
2 _____
3 _____
4 _____
5 _____

DAILY AFFIRMATIONS (Page 37)
I am doing my self-affirmations tomorrow at the following times.

1)_____ 2)_____ 3)_____

'SMILE' (Page 125)
Smile at yourself in the mirror, and be proud, you've done your best!
I'm smiling at my self tomorrow 3 times at the following times:

1)_____ 2)_____ 3)_____

PRESS THE ANTI-STRESS BUTTON (Page 50)
When will I take my 3 x 2 minute breaks tomorrow?

1)_____ 2)_____ 3)_____

GET OFF YOUR BOTTOM (Page 99)
No drug can replace the benefits of exercise. So tomorrow I'm going to:
_____

GRATEFULL THINGS (Page 94)
What are the 3 things I am most grateful for today?

1 _____
2 _____
3 _____

Day   Date   The 5 Minute Focus

Quote...

"The ones who are crazy enough to think they can change the world, are the ones who do." Anon

PRODUCTIVE THINGS (Page 108)
What are the 5 most productive things I can do tomorrow?

1 _____
2 _____
3 _____
4 _____
5 _____

DAILY AFFIRMATIONS (Page 37)
I am doing my self-affirmations tomorrow at the following times.

1)_____ 2)_____ 3) _____

HAPPINESS 'REFRAME' (Page 86)
If anything pops into my head to annoy me I will simply deal with it, let it go, or think about it from a new perspective. My new perspective tomorrow is:

_____

PRESS THE ANTI-STRESS BUTTON (Page 50)
When will I take my 3 x 2 minute breaks tomorrow?

1)_____ 2)_____ 3) _____

GET OFF YOUR BOTTOM (Page 99)
No drug can replace the benefits of exercise. So tomorrow I'm going to:

_____

GRATEFULL THINGS (Page 94)
What are the 3 things I am most grateful for today?

1 _____
2 _____
3 _____

Day   Date   The 5 Minute Focus

Quote...

"Courage is resistance to fear, mastery of fear, not absence of fear." Mark Twain

GET IN THE FLOW THIS WEEKEND (Page 127)

Try your own ideas, were all so different (or a few of the following) Listen to music. Visit a really good friend. Read a book. Cook something new. Get a cuddle. Plan your dreams. Plan your week ensuring you do things you enjoy. Tidy your environment. Try a new task or hobby. Go somewhere different. Seek out some laughter (even on the tele) or in good company. Engage in a new hobby or sport. Gardening, yes this actually appeals to some. Golf, tennis, a walk or your favourite hobby, in fact anything you gain pleasure from. My FLOW task this weekend is

___

DAILY AFFIRMATIONS (Page 37)
I am doing my self-affirmations tomorrow at the following times.
1)_____ 2)_____ 3) _____

"AS IF" (Page 35)
Blow yourself up a bit and believe it, you can hold any state you want. Just colourfully visualise the state you wish for and make it happen in reality. Today I will behave as if...

___

DON'T OVERTHINK BE HAPPY (Page 90)
Stop overthinking and ruminating trust it will all turn out OK.
I'm thinking optimistically tomorrow about:

___

GET OFF YOUR BOTTOM (Page 99)
No drug can replace the benefits of exercise. So tomorrow I'm going to:

___

GRATEFULL THINGS (Page 94)
What are the 3 things I am most grateful for today?

1 _____
2 _____
3 _____

Day   Date   The 5 Minute Focus

Quote...

"We become what we think about most of the time, and that's the strangest secret." **Earl Nightingale**

KINDNESS (Page 96)

I will spread some kindness tomorrow by doing these 5 things; of course you can spread these through the week if you wish.

1. _____
2. _____
3. _____
4. _____
5. _____

SAVOURING (Page 130)

Slow down, live in the moment. Tomorrow I look forward to savouring:

_____

THREE GOOD THINGS (Page 115)

What 3 good things happened today?

1. _____
2. _____
3. _____

PRESS THE ANTI-STRESS BUTTON (Page 50)

When will I take my 3 x 2 minute breaks tomorrow?

1) _____ 2) _____ 3) _____

GET OFF YOUR BOTTOM (Page 99)

No drug can replace the benefits of exercise. So tomorrow I'm going to:

_____

GRATEFULL THINGS (Page 94)

What are the 3 things I am most grateful for today?

1. _____
2. _____
3. _____

Day   Date   (Maybe Sunday?)   The 5 Minute Focus

Quote...
"Success is liking yourself, liking what you do, and liking how you do it." **Maya Angelou**

GOALS AND DREAMS (Page 109)
What goals and dreams can I imagine?

_____
_____
_____

WHAT STEPS DO I NEED TO TAKE TO GET THERE (Page 40)
Imagine and picture your 'BEST POSSIBLE SELF'

_____
_____
_____

PRODUCTIVE THINGS (Page 108)
What are the 5 most productive things I can do tomorrow?

1 _____
2 _____
3 _____
4 _____
5 _____

PRESS THE ANTI-STRESS BUTTON (Page 50)

When will I take my 3 x 2 minute breaks tomorrow?
1)_____ 2)_____ 3)_____

GET OFF YOUR BOTTOM (Page 99)
No drug can replace the benefits of exercise. So tomorrow I'm going to:

_____

GRATEFULL THINGS (Page 94)
What are the 3 things I am most grateful for today?

1 _____
2 _____
3 _____

Day   Date   The 5 Minute Focus

Quote...

"Develop success from failures. Discouragement and failure are two of the surest stepping stones to success"
Dale Carnegie

PRODUCTIVE THINGS (Page 108)
What are the 5 most productive things I can do tomorrow?

1. _____
2. _____
3. _____
4. _____
5. _____

DAILY AFFIRMATIONS (Page 37)
I am doing my self-affirmations tomorrow at the following times.

1) _____ 2) _____ 3) _____

SAVOURING (Page 130)
Slow down, live in the moment. Tomorrow I look forward to savouring, these 3 things.

1. _____
2. _____
3. _____

PRESS THE ANTI-STRESS BUTTON (Page 50)
When will I take my 3 x 2 minute breaks tomorrow?

1) _____ 2) _____ 3) _____

GET OFF YOUR BOTTOM (Page 99)
No drug can replace the benefits of exercise. So tomorrow I'm going to:

_____

GRATEFULL THINGS (Page 94)
What are the 3 things I am most grateful for today?

1. _____
2. _____
3. _____

Day   Date   The 5 Minute Focus

Quote...
"The starting point of all achievement is desire."
Napoleon Hill

PRODUCTIVE THINGS (Page 108)
What are the 5 most productive things I can do tomorrow?

1 _____
2 _____
3 _____
4 _____
5 _____

DAILY AFFIRMATIONS (Page 37)
I am doing my self-affirmations tomorrow at the following times.

1) _____ 2) _____ 3) _____

KARMA (Page 44)
'What goes around comes around'
My small favour for someone else today is:

_____

PRESS THE ANTI-STRESS BUTTON (Page 50)
When will I take my 3 x 2 minute breaks tomorrow?

1) _____ 2) _____ 3) _____

GET OFF YOUR BOTTOM (Page 99)
No drug can replace the benefits of exercise. So tomorrow I'm going to:

_____

GRATEFULL THINGS (Page 94)
What are the 3 things I am most grateful for today?

1 _____
2 _____
3 _____

Day   Date   The 5 Minute Focus

Quote...

"I find that the harder I work, the more luck I seem to have." **Thomas Jefferson**

PRODUCTIVE THINGS (Page 108)
What are the 5 most productive things I can do tomorrow?

1 _____
2 _____
3 _____
4 _____
5 _____

DAILY AFFIRMATIONS (Page 37)
I am doing my self-affirmations tomorrow at the following times.

1) _____ 2) _____ 3) _____

'SMILE' (Page 125)
Smile at yourself in the mirror, and be proud, you've done your best!
I'm smiling at my self tomorrow 3 times at the following times:

1) _____ 2) _____ 3) _____

PRESS THE ANTI-STRESS BUTTON (Page 50)
When will I take my 3 x 2 minute breaks tomorrow?
1) _____ 2) _____ 3) _____

GET OFF YOUR BOTTOM (Page 99)
No drug can replace the benefits of exercise. So tomorrow I'm going to:

_____

GRATEFULL THINGS (Page 94)
What are the 3 things I am most grateful for today?

1 _____
2 _____
3 _____

Day   Date   The 5 Minute Focus

Quote...

"I believe that the only courage anybody ever needs is the courage to follow your own dreams." **Oprah Winfrey**

PRODUCTIVE THINGS (Page 108)
What are the 5 most productive things I can do tomorrow?

1 _____
2 _____
3 _____
4 _____
5 _____

DAILY AFFIRMATIONS (Page 37)
I am doing my self-affirmations tomorrow at the following times.

1) _____ 2) _____ 3) _____

HAPPINESS 'REFRAME' (Page 86)
If anything pops into my head to annoy me I will simply deal with it, let it go, or think about it from a new perspective. My new perspective tomorrow is:

_____

PRESS THE ANTI-STRESS BUTTON (Page 50)
When will I take my 3 x 2 minute breaks tomorrow?

1) _____ 2) _____ 3) _____

GET OFF YOUR BOTTOM (Page 99)
No drug can replace the benefits of exercise. So tomorrow I'm going to:

_____

GRATEFULL THINGS (Page 94)
What are the 3 things I am most grateful for today?

1 _____
2 _____
3 _____

Day   Date   The 5 Minute Focus

Quote...
"There are two types of people who will tell you that you cannot make a difference in this world, those who are afraid to try and those who are afraid you will succeed." **Ray Goforth**
GET IN THE FLOW THIS WEEKEND (Page 127)

Try your own ideas, were all so different (or a few of the following) Listen to music. Visit a really good friend. Read a book. Cook something new. Get a cuddle. Plan your dreams. Plan your week ensuring you do things you enjoy. Tidy your environment. Try a new task or hobby. Go somewhere different. Seek out some laughter (even on the tele) or in good company. Engage in a new hobby or sport. Gardening, yes this actually appeals to some. Golf, tennis, a walk or your favourite hobby, in fact anything you gain pleasure from. My FLOW task this weekend is

---

DAILY AFFIRMATIONS (Page 37)
I am doing my self-affirmations tomorrow at the following times.
1)_____ 2)_____ 3) _____

"AS IF" (Page 35)
Blow yourself up a bit and believe it, you can hold any state you want. Just colourfully visualise the state you wish for and make it happen in reality. Today I will behave as if...

DON'T OVERTHINK BE HAPPY (Page 90)
Stop overthinking and ruminating trust it will all turn out OK.
I'm thinking optimistically tomorrow about:

GET OFF YOUR BOTTOM (Page 99)
No drug can replace the benefits of exercise. So tomorrow I'm going to:

GRATEFULL THINGS (Page 94)
What are the 3 things I am most grateful for today?
1 _____
2 _____
3 _____

Day   Date   The 5 Minute Focus

Quote...

"Optimism is the faith that leads to achievement."
Helen Keller

KINDNESS (Page 96)
I will spread some kindness tomorrow by doing these 5 things; of course you can spread these through the week if you wish.

1 _____
2 _____
3 _____
4 _____
5 _____

SAVOURING (Page 130)
Slow down, live in the moment. Tomorrow I look forward to savouring:

_____

THREE GOOD THINGS (Page 115)
What 3 good things happened today?

1 _____
2 _____
3 _____

PRESS THE ANTI-STRESS BUTTON (Page 50)
When will I take my 3 x 2 minute breaks tomorrow?

1) _____   2) _____   3) _____

GET OFF YOUR BOTTOM (Page 99)
No drug can replace the benefits of exercise. So tomorrow I'm going to:

_____

GRATEFULL THINGS (Page 94)
What are the 3 things I am most grateful for today?

1 _____
2 _____
3 _____

Day Date (Maybe Sunday?) The 5 Minute Focus

Quote...

"When you stop chasing the wrong things, you give the right things a chance to catch you." **Lolly Daskal**

GOALS AND DREAMS (Page 109)
What goals and dreams can I imagine?

_____
_____
_____

WHAT STEPS DO I NEED TO TAKE TO GET THERE (Page 40)
Imagine and picture your 'BEST POSSIBLE SELF'

_____
_____
_____

PRODUCTIVE THINGS (Page 108)
What are the 5 most productive things I can do tomorrow?

1 _____
2 _____
3 _____
4 _____
5 _____

PRESS THE ANTI-STRESS BUTTON (Page 50)
When will I take my 3 x 2 minute breaks tomorrow?

1) _____ 2) _____ 3) _____

GET OFF YOUR BOTTOM (Page 99)
No drug can replace the benefits of exercise. So tomorrow I'm going to:

_____

GRATEFULL THINGS (Page 94)
What are the 3 things I am most grateful for today?

1 _____
2 _____
3 _____

Day   Date   The 5 Minute Focus

Quote...

"Our greatest weakness lies in giving up. The most certain way to succeed is always to try just one more time."
Thomas A. Edison

PRODUCTIVE THINGS (Page 108)
What are the 5 most productive things I can do tomorrow?

1 _____
2 _____
3 _____
4 _____
5 _____

DAILY AFFIRMATIONS (Page 37)
I am doing my self-affirmations tomorrow at the following times.

1) _____   2) _____   3) _____

SAVOURING (Page 130)
Slow down, live in the moment. Tomorrow I look forward to savouring, these 3 things.

1 _____
2 _____
3 _____

PRESS THE ANTI-STRESS BUTTON (Page 50)
When will I take my 3 x 2 minute breaks tomorrow?

1) _____   2) _____   3) _____

GET OFF YOUR BOTTOM (Page 99)
No drug can replace the benefits of exercise. So tomorrow I'm going to:

_____
_____

GRATEFULL THINGS (Page 94)
What are the 3 things I am most grateful for today?

1 _____
2 _____
3 _____

Day   Date   The 5 Minute Focus

Quote...

"Nobody who ever gave his best regretted it."
George Halas

PRODUCTIVE THINGS (Page 108)
What are the 5 most productive things I can do tomorrow?

1 _____
2 _____
3 _____
4 _____
5 _____

DAILY AFFIRMATIONS (Page 37)
I am doing my self-affirmations tomorrow at the following times.

1) _____ 2) _____ 3) _____

KARMA (Page 44)
'What goes around comes around'
My small favour for someone else today is:

PRESS THE ANTI-STRESS BUTTON (Page 50)
When will I take my 3 x 2 minute breaks tomorrow?

1) _____ 2) _____ 3) _____

GET OFF YOUR BOTTOM (Page 99)
No drug can replace the benefits of exercise. So tomorrow I'm going to:

GRATEFULL THINGS (Page 94)
What are the 3 things I am most grateful for today?

1 _____
2 _____
3 _____

Day   Date   The 5 Minute Focus

Quote...

"It is the mark of an educated mind to be able to entertain a thought without accepting it." **Aristotle**

PRODUCTIVE THINGS (Page 108)
What are the 5 most productive things I can do tomorrow?

1 _____
2 _____
3 _____
4 _____
5 _____

DAILY AFFIRMATIONS (Page 37)
I am doing my self-affirmations tomorrow at the following times.

1) _____   2) _____   3) _____

'SMILE' (Page 125)
Smile at yourself in the mirror, and be proud, you've done your best!
I'm smiling at my self tomorrow 3 times at the following times:

1) _____   2) _____   3) _____

PRESS THE ANTI-STRESS BUTTON (Page 50)
When will I take my 3 x 2 minute breaks tomorrow?

1) _____   2) _____   3) _____

GET OFF YOUR BOTTOM (Page 99)
No drug can replace the benefits of exercise. So tomorrow I'm going to:

_____

GRATEFULL THINGS (Page 94)
What are the 3 things I am most grateful for today?

1 _____
2 _____
3 _____

Day   Date   The 5 Minute Focus

Quote...

"Most men die at 25... we just don't bury them until they are 70." - Benjamin Franklin

PRODUCTIVE THINGS (Page 108)
What are the 5 most productive things I can do tomorrow?

1. _____
2. _____
3. _____
4. _____
5. _____

DAILY AFFIRMATIONS (Page 37)
I am doing my self-affirmations tomorrow at the following times.

1) _____ 2) _____ 3) _____

HAPPINESS 'REFRAME' (Page 86)
If anything pops into my head to annoy me I will simply deal with it, let it go, or think about it from a new perspective. My new perspective tomorrow is:

_____

PRESS THE ANTI-STRESS BUTTON (Page 50)
When will I take my 3 x 2 minute breaks tomorrow?

1) _____ 2) _____ 3) _____

GET OFF YOUR BOTTOM (Page 99)
No drug can replace the benefits of exercise. So tomorrow I'm going to:

_____

GRATEFULL THINGS (Page 94)
What are the 3 things I am most grateful for today?

1. _____
2. _____
3. _____

Day   Date   The 5 Minute Focus

Quote...
"You will never do anything in this world without courage. It is the greatest quality of the mind next to honor." **Aristotle**

GET IN THE FLOW THIS WEEKEND (Page 127)

Try your own ideas, were all so different (or a few of the following) Listen to music. Visit a really good friend. Read a book. Cook something new. Get a cuddle. Plan your dreams. Plan your week ensuring you do things you enjoy. Tidy your environment. Try a new task or hobby. Go somewhere different. Seek out some laughter (even on the tele) or in good company. Engage in a new hobby or sport. Gardening, yes this actually appeals to some. Golf, tennis, a walk or your favourite hobby, in fact anything you gain pleasure from. My FLOW task this weekend is

---

DAILY AFFIRMATIONS (Page 37)
I am doing my self-affirmations tomorrow at the following times.
1)_____ 2)_____ 3) _____

"AS IF" (Page 35)
Blow yourself up a bit and believe it, you can hold any state you want. Just colourfully visualise the state you wish for and make it happen in reality. Today I will behave as if...

DON'T OVERTHINK BE HAPPY (Page 90)
Stop overthinking and ruminating trust it will all turn out OK.
I'm thinking optimistically tomorrow about:

GET OFF YOUR BOTTOM (Page 99)
No drug can replace the benefits of exercise. So tomorrow I'm going to:

GRATEFULL THINGS (Page 94)
What are the 3 things I am most grateful for today?

1 _____
2 _____
3 _____

Day   Date   The 5 Minute Focus

Quote...

"The eye only see's what the mind is prepared to comprehend" **Henri Bergson**

KINDNESS (Page 96)
I will spread some kindness tomorrow by doing these 5 things; of course you can spread these through the week if you wish.

1 _____
2 _____
3 _____
4 _____
5 _____

SAVOURING (Page 130)
Slow down, live in the moment. Tomorrow I look forward to savouring:

_____

THREE GOOD THINGS (Page 115)
What 3 good things happened today?

1 _____
2 _____
3 _____

PRESS THE ANTI-STRESS BUTTON (Page 50)
When will I take my 3 x 2 minute breaks tomorrow?

1) _____ 2) _____ 3) _____

GET OFF YOUR BOTTOM (Page 99)
No drug can replace the benefits of exercise. So tomorrow I'm going to:

_____

GRATEFULL THINGS (Page 94)
What are the 3 things I am most grateful for today?

1 _____
2 _____
3 _____

Day   Date   (Maybe Sunday?) The 5 Minute Focus

Quote...

"It doesn't matter where you are coming from. All that matters is where you are going." **Brian Tracy**

GOALS AND DREAMS (Page 109)
What goals and dreams can I imagine?

_____
_____
_____

WHAT STEPS DO I NEED TO TAKE TO GET THERE (Page 40)
Imagine and picture your 'BEST POSSIBLE SELF'

_____
_____

PRODUCTIVE THINGS (Page 108)
What are the 5 most productive things I can do tomorrow?

1 _____
2 _____
3 _____
4 _____
5 _____

PRESS THE ANTI-STRESS BUTTON (Page 50)
When will I take my 3 x 2 minute breaks tomorrow?

1) _____ 2) _____ 3) _____

GET OFF YOUR BOTTOM (Page 99)
No drug can replace the benefits of exercise. So tomorrow I'm going to:

_____

GRATEFULL THINGS (Page 94)
What are the 3 things I am most grateful for today?

1 _____
2 _____
3 _____

Day　　　　　　Date　　　　　　The 5 Minute Focus

Quote...

"Failure isn't Fatal... but Failure to Change could be!"
John Wooden

PRODUCTIVE THINGS (Page 108)
What are the 5 most productive things I can do tomorrow?

1. _____
2. _____
3. _____
4. _____
5. _____

DAILY AFFIRMATIONS (Page 37)
I am doing my self-affirmations tomorrow at the following times.

1) _____ 2) _____ 3) _____

SAVOURING (Page 130)
Slow down, live in the moment. Tomorrow I look forward to savouring, these 3 things.

1. _____
2. _____
3. _____

PRESS THE ANTI-STRESS BUTTON (Page 50)
When will I take my 3 x 2 minute breaks tomorrow?

1) _____ 2) _____ 3) _____

GET OFF YOUR BOTTOM (Page 99)
No drug can replace the benefits of exercise. So tomorrow I'm going to:

_____

GRATEFULL THINGS (Page 94)
What are the 3 things I am most grateful for today?

1. _____
2. _____
3. _____

Day   Date   The 5 Minute Focus

Quote...
"No man has a good enough memory to be a successful liar. " Abraham Lincoln

PRODUCTIVE THINGS (Page 108)
What are the 5 most productive things I can do tomorrow?

1 _____
2 _____
3 _____
4 _____
5 _____

DAILY AFFIRMATIONS (Page 37)
I am doing my self-affirmations tomorrow at the following times.

1) _____   2) _____   3) _____

KARMA (Page 44)
'What goes around comes around'
My small favour for someone else today is:

_____

PRESS THE ANTI-STRESS BUTTON (Page 50)
When will I take my 3 x 2 minute breaks tomorrow?

1) _____   2) _____   3) _____

GET OFF YOUR BOTTOM (Page 99)
No drug can replace the benefits of exercise. So tomorrow I'm going to:

_____

GRATEFULL THINGS (Page 94)
What are the 3 things I am most grateful for today?

1 _____
2 _____
3 _____

Day   Date   The 5 Minute Focus

Quote...

"Think big and don't listen to people who tell you it can't be done. Life's to short to think small." Tim Ferris

PRODUCTIVE THINGS (Page 108)
What are the 5 most productive things I can do tomorrow?

1 _____
2 _____
3 _____
4 _____
5 _____

DAILY AFFIRMATIONS (Page 37)
I am doing my self-affirmations tomorrow at the following times.

1) _____ 2) _____ 3) _____

'SMILE' (Page 125)
Smile at yourself in the mirror, and be proud, you've done your best!
I'm smiling at my self tomorrow 3 times at the following times:

1) _____ 2) _____ 3) _____

PRESS THE ANTI-STRESS BUTTON (Page 50)
When will I take my 3 x 2 minute breaks tomorrow?

1) _____ 2) _____ 3) _____

GET OFF YOUR BOTTOM (Page 99)
No drug can replace the benefits of exercise. So tomorrow I'm going to:

_____

GRATEFULL THINGS (Page 94)
What are the 3 things I am most grateful for today?

1 _____
2 _____
3 _____

Day   Date   The 5 Minute Focus

Quote...

"Change you thoughts and your thoughts change the world." **Norman Vincent Peale**

PRODUCTIVE THINGS (Page 108)
What are the 5 most productive things I can do tomorrow?

1 _____
2 _____
3 _____
4 _____
5 _____

DAILY AFFIRMATIONS (Page 37)
I am doing my self-affirmations tomorrow at the following times.

1)_____ 2)_____ 3)_____

HAPPINESS 'REFRAME' (Page 86)
If anything pops into my head to annoy me I will simply deal with it, let it go, or think about it from a new perspective. My new perspective tomorrow is:

_____

PRESS THE ANTI-STRESS BUTTON (Page 50)
When will I take my 3 x 2 minute breaks tomorrow?

1)_____ 2)_____ 3)_____

GET OFF YOUR BOTTOM (Page 99)
No drug can replace the benefits of exercise. So tomorrow I'm going to:

_____

GRATEFULL THINGS (Page 94)
What are the 3 things I am most grateful for today?

1 _____
2 _____
3 _____

Day   Date   The 5 Minute Focus

Quote...

"Everything you have ever wanted is on the other side of fear." George Addair

GET IN THE FLOW THIS WEEKEND (Page 127)

Try your own ideas, were all so different (or a few of the following) Listen to music. Visit a really good friend. Read a book. Cook something new. Get a cuddle. Plan your dreams. Plan your week ensuring you do things you enjoy. Tidy your environment. Try a new task or hobby. Go somewhere different. Seek out some laughter (even on the tele) or in good company. Engage in a new hobby or sport. Gardening, yes this actually appeals to some. Golf, tennis, a walk or your favourite hobby, in fact anything you gain pleasure from. My FLOW task this weekend is

---

DAILY AFFIRMATIONS (Page 37)
I am doing my self-affirmations tomorrow at the following times.
1)_____ 2)_____ 3) _____

"AS IF" (Page 35)
Blow yourself up a bit and believe it, you can hold any state you want. Just colourfully visualise the state you wish for and make it happen in reality. Today I will behave as if...

DON'T OVERTHINK BE HAPPY (Page 90)
Stop overthinking and ruminating trust it will all turn out OK.
I'm thinking optimistically tomorrow about:

GET OFF YOUR BOTTOM (Page 99)
No drug can replace the benefits of exercise. So tomorrow I'm going to:

GRATEFULL THINGS (Page 94)
What are the 3 things I am most grateful for today?

1 _____
2 _____
3 _____

Day   Date   The 5 Minute Focus

Quote...

"Making a big life change is pretty scary. But know what's even scarier? Regret." Zig Ziglar

KINDNESS (Page 96)
I will spread some kindness tomorrow by doing these 5 things; of course you can spread these through the week if you wish.

1. _____
2. _____
3. _____
4. _____
5. _____

SAVOURING (Page 130)
Slow down, live in the moment. Tomorrow I look forward to savouring:

_____

THREE GOOD THINGS (Page 115)
What 3 good things happened today?

1. _____
2. _____
3. _____

PRESS THE ANTI-STRESS BUTTON (Page 50)
When will I take my 3 x 2 minute breaks tomorrow?

1) _____ 2) _____ 3) _____

GET OFF YOUR BOTTOM (Page 99)
No drug can replace the benefits of exercise. So tomorrow I'm going to:

_____

GRATEFULL THINGS (Page 94)
What are the 3 things I am most grateful for today?

1. _____
2. _____
3. _____

Day   Date   (Maybe Sunday?) The 5 Minute Focus

Quote...

"Our lives begin to end the day we become silent about things that matter. " **Martin Luthor King JR**

GOALS AND DREAMS (Page 109)
What goals and dreams can I imagine?

_____

_____

_____

WHAT STEPS DO I NEED TO TAKE TO GET THERE (Page 40)
Imagine and picture your 'BEST POSSIBLE SELF'

_____

_____

_____

PRODUCTIVE THINGS (Page 108)
What are the 5 most productive things I can do tomorrow?

1 _____
2 _____
3 _____
4 _____
5 _____

PRESS THE ANTI-STRESS BUTTON (Page 50)
When will I take my 3 x 2 minute breaks tomorrow?

1) _____ 2) _____ 3) _____

GET OFF YOUR BOTTOM (Page 99)
No drug can replace the benefits of exercise. So tomorrow I'm going to:

_____

GRATEFULL THINGS (Page 94)
What are the 3 things I am most grateful for today?

1 _____
2 _____
3 _____

SELF-AFFIRMATIONS
YOUR CHANCE FOR A REVIEW, ANY ADJUSTMENTS NEEDED OR ALL COOL? 😊😊

We build up feelings of security or insecurity by how we think. The power of thought is exceptionally influential on our feelings and emotions. What we are simply doing here is training your brain to go in the direction YOU have chosen it to go in, rather than let it wander where it likes. See the chapter beginning on Page 37 on how to construct these.

My self-affirmations for next month are:

_____

_____

_____

_____

_____

_____

_____

_____

_____

_____

_____

_____

_____

_____

_____

_____

_____

_____

Day   Date   The 5 Minute Focus

Quote...

"The only place where success comes before work is in the dictionary." **Vidal Sassoon**

PRODUCTIVE THINGS (Page 108)
What are the 5 most productive things I can do tomorrow?

1 _____
2 _____
3 _____
4 _____
5 _____

DAILY AFFIRMATIONS (Page 37)
I am doing my self-affirmations tomorrow at the following times.

1) _____ 2) _____ 3) _____

SAVOURING (Page 130)
Slow down, live in the moment. Tomorrow I look forward to savouring, these 3 things.

1 _____
2 _____
3 _____

PRESS THE ANTI-STRESS BUTTON (Page 50)
When will I take my 3 x 2 minute breaks tomorrow?

1) _____ 2) _____ 3) _____

GET OFF YOUR BOTTOM (Page 99)
No drug can replace the benefits of exercise. So tomorrow I'm going to:

_____

GRATEFULL THINGS (Page 94)
What are the 3 things I am most grateful for today?

1 _____
2 _____
3 _____

Day   Date   The 5 Minute Focus

Quote...
"To affect the quality of the day, that is the highest of arts."
Henry David Thoreau

PRODUCTIVE THINGS (Page 108)
What are the 5 most productive things I can do tomorrow?

1 _____
2 _____
3 _____
4 _____
5 _____

DAILY AFFIRMATIONS (Page 37)
I am doing my self-affirmations tomorrow at the following times.

1) _____   2) _____   3) _____

KARMA (Page 44)
'What goes around comes around'
My small favour for someone else today is:

_____

PRESS THE ANTI-STRESS BUTTON (Page 50)
When will I take my 3 x 2 minute breaks tomorrow?

1) _____   2) _____   3) _____

GET OFF YOUR BOTTOM (Page 99)
No drug can replace the benefits of exercise. So tomorrow I'm going to:

_____

GRATEFULL THINGS (Page 94)
What are the 3 things I am most grateful for today?

1 _____
2 _____
3 _____

Day   Date   The 5 Minute Focus

Quote...

"I am thankful for all those who said, 'No' to me. It's because of them I'm doing myself." **Albert Einstein**

PRODUCTIVE THINGS (Page 108)
What are the 5 most productive things I can do tomorrow?

1. _____
2. _____
3. _____
4. _____
5. _____

DAILY AFFIRMATIONS (Page 37)
I am doing my self-affirmations tomorrow at the following times.

1) _____ 2) _____ 3) _____

'SMILE' (Page 125)
Smile at yourself in the mirror, and be proud, you've done your best!
I'm smiling at my self tomorrow 3 times at the following times:

1) _____ 2) _____ 3) _____

PRESS THE ANTI-STRESS BUTTON (Page 50)
When will I take my 3 x 2 minute breaks tomorrow?

1) _____ 2) _____ 3) _____

GET OFF YOUR BOTTOM (Page 99)
No drug can replace the benefits of exercise. So tomorrow I'm going to:

_____
_____

GRATEFULL THINGS (Page 94)
What are the 3 things I am most grateful for today?

1. _____
2. _____
3. _____

Day   Date   The 5 Minute Focus

Quote...
"Gratitude can transform common days into thanksgivings, turn routine jobs into joy, and change ordinary opportunities into blessings" W A Ward

PRODUCTIVE THINGS (Page 108)
What are the 5 most productive things I can do tomorrow?

1 _____
2 _____
3 _____
4 _____
5 _____

DAILY AFFIRMATIONS (Page 37)
I am doing my self-affirmations tomorrow at the following times.

1) _____   2) _____   3) _____

HAPPINESS 'REFRAME' (Page 86)
If anything pops into my head to annoy me I will simply deal with it, let it go, or think about it from a new perspective. My new perspective tomorrow is:

PRESS THE ANTI-STRESS BUTTON (Page 50)
When will I take my 3 x 2 minute breaks tomorrow?

1) _____   2) _____   3) _____

GET OFF YOUR BOTTOM (Page 99)
No drug can replace the benefits of exercise. So tomorrow I'm going to:

GRATEFULL THINGS (Page 94)
What are the 3 things I am most grateful for today?

1 _____
2 _____
3 _____

Day   Date   The 5 Minute Focus

Quote...
"Don't be too timid and squeamish about your actions. All life is an experiment. The more experiments you make the better."- **Ralph Waldo Emerson**

GET IN THE FLOW THIS WEEKEND (Page 127)

Try your own ideas, were all so different (or a few of the following) Listen to music. Visit a really good friend. Read a book. Cook something new. Get a cuddle. Plan your dreams. Plan your week ensuring you do things you enjoy. Tidy your environment. Try a new task or hobby. Go somewhere different. Seek out some laughter (even on the tele) or in good company. Engage in a new hobby or sport. Gardening, yes this actually appeals to some. Golf, tennis, a walk or your favourite hobby, in fact anything you gain pleasure from. My FLOW task this weekend is

---

DAILY AFFIRMATIONS (Page 37)
I am doing my self-affirmations tomorrow at the following times.
1)_____ 2)_____ 3) _____

"AS IF" (Page 35)
Blow yourself up a bit and believe it, you can hold any state you want. Just colourfully visualise the state you wish for and make it happen in reality. Today I will behave as if

---

DON'T OVERTHINK BE HAPPY (Page 90)
Stop overthinking and ruminating trust it will all turn out OK.
I'm thinking optimistically tomorrow about:

GET OFF YOUR BOTTOM (Page 99)
No drug can replace the benefits of exercise. So tomorrow I'm going to:

GRATEFULL THINGS (Page 94)
What are the 3 things I am most grateful for today?

1 _____
2 _____
3 _____

Day   Date   The 5 Minute Focus

Quote...

"You will never change your life until you change something you do daily. The secret of your success is found in your daily routine" **John C Maxwell**

KINDNESS (Page 96)
I will spread some kindness tomorrow by doing these 5 things; of course you can spread these through the week if you wish.

1 _____
2 _____
3 _____
4 _____
5 _____

SAVOURING (Page 130)
Slow down, live in the moment. Tomorrow I look forward to savouring:

_____

THREE GOOD THINGS (Page 115)
What 3 good things happened today?

1 _____
2 _____
3 _____

PRESS THE ANTI-STRESS BUTTON (Page 50)
When will I take my 3 x 2 minute breaks tomorrow?

1) _____   2) _____   3) _____

GET OFF YOUR BOTTOM (Page 99)
No drug can replace the benefits of exercise. So tomorrow I'm going to:

_____

GRATEFULL THINGS (Page 94)
What are the 3 things I am most grateful for today?

1 _____
2 _____
3 _____

Day   Date   (Maybe Sunday?) The 5 Minute Focus

Quote...

"We don't rise to the level of our expectations we fall to the level of our training" **Archilochos**

GOALS AND DREAMS (Page 109)
What goals and dreams can I imagine?

_____

_____

_____

WHAT STEPS DO I NEED TO TAKE TO GET THERE (Page 40)
Imagine and picture your 'BEST POSSIBLE SELF'

_____

_____

PRODUCTIVE THINGS (Page 108)
What are the 5 most productive things I can do tomorrow?

1 _____
2 _____
3 _____
4 _____
5 _____

PRESS THE ANTI-STRESS BUTTON (Page 50)
When will I take my 3 x 2 minute breaks tomorrow?

1)_____ 2)_____ 3) _____

GET OFF YOUR BOTTOM (Page 99)
No drug can replace the benefits of exercise. So tomorrow I'm going to:

_____

GRATEFULL THINGS (Page 94)
What are the 3 things I am most grateful for today?

1 _____
2 _____
3 _____

Day   Date   The 5 Minute Focus

Quote...

"It's never too late to redefine self-control to change long ingrained habits, and to do the work your capable of."
Seth Godin

PRODUCTIVE THINGS (Page 108)
What are the 5 most productive things I can do tomorrow?

1 _____
2 _____
3 _____
4 _____
5 _____

DAILY AFFIRMATIONS (Page 37)
I am doing my self-affirmations tomorrow at the following times.

1) _____   2) _____   3) _____

SAVOURING (Page 130)
Slow down, live in the moment. Tomorrow I look forward to savouring, these 3 things.

1 _____
2 _____
3 _____

PRESS THE ANTI-STRESS BUTTON (Page 50)
When will I take my 3 x 2 minute breaks tomorrow?

1) _____   2) _____   3) _____

GET OFF YOUR BOTTOM (Page 99)
No drug can replace the benefits of exercise. So tomorrow I'm going to:

_____

GRATEFULL THINGS (Page 94)
What are the 3 things I am most grateful for today?

1 _____
2 _____
3 _____

Day   Date   The 5 Minute Focus

Quote...

"If you don't like it you've two options. Change it, or come to terms with it by looking at it differently" **Martin Hill**

PRODUCTIVE THINGS (Page 108)
What are the 5 most productive things I can do tomorrow?

1 _____
2 _____
3 _____
4 _____
5 _____

DAILY AFFIRMATIONS (Page 37)
I am doing my self-affirmations tomorrow at the following times.

1)_____ 2)_____ 3)_____

KARMA (Page 44)
'What goes around comes around'
My small favour for someone else today is:

PRESS THE ANTI-STRESS BUTTON (Page 50)
When will I take my 3 x 2 minute breaks tomorrow?

1)_____ 2)_____ 3)_____

GET OFF YOUR BOTTOM (Page 99)
No drug can replace the benefits of exercise. So tomorrow I'm going to:

GRATEFULL THINGS (Page 94)
What are the 3 things I am most grateful for today?

1 _____
2 _____
3 _____

Day   Date   The 5 Minute Focus

Quote...

"As a cure for worrying work is better than whiskey."
Thomas Edison

PRODUCTIVE THINGS (Page 108)
What are the 5 most productive things I can do tomorrow?

1 _____
2 _____
3 _____
4 _____
5 _____

DAILY AFFIRMATIONS (Page 37)
I am doing my self-affirmations tomorrow at the following times.

1)_____ 2)_____ 3)_____

'SMILE' (Page 125)
Smile at yourself in the mirror, and be proud, you've done your best!
I'm smiling at my self tomorrow 3 times at the following times:

1)_____ 2)_____ 3)_____

PRESS THE ANTI-STRESS BUTTON (Page 50)
When will I take my 3 x 2 minute breaks tomorrow?

1)_____ 2)_____ 3)_____

GET OFF YOUR BOTTOM (Page 99)
No drug can replace the benefits of exercise. So tomorrow I'm going to:

_____

GRATEFULL THINGS (Page 94)
What are the 3 things I am most grateful for today?

1 _____
2 _____
3 _____

Day   Date   The 5 Minute Focus

Quote...

"What you do today can improve all your tomorrows" **Ralph Marston**

PRODUCTIVE THINGS (Page 108)
What are the 5 most productive things I can do tomorrow?

1 _____
2 _____
3 _____
4 _____
5 _____

DAILY AFFIRMATIONS (Page 37)
I am doing my self-affirmations tomorrow at the following times.

1) _____ 2) _____ 3) _____

HAPPINESS 'REFRAME' (Page 86)
If anything pops into my head to annoy me I will simply deal with it, let it go, or think about it from a new perspective. My new perspective tomorrow is:

_____

PRESS THE ANTI-STRESS BUTTON (Page 50)
When will I take my 3 x 2 minute breaks tomorrow?

1) _____ 2) _____ 3) _____

GET OFF YOUR BOTTOM (Page 99)
No drug can replace the benefits of exercise. So tomorrow I'm going to:

_____

GRATEFULL THINGS (Page 94)
What are the 3 things I am most grateful for today?

1 _____
2 _____
3 _____

Day   Date   The 5 Minute Focus

Quote...
"Change your thoughts and your thoughts change your world" **Norman Vincent Peal.**
(repeated because it's a favourite)

GET IN THE FLOW THIS WEEKEND (Page 127)

Try your own ideas, were all so different (or a few of the following) Listen to music. Visit a really good friend. Read a book. Cook something new. Get a cuddle. Plan your dreams. Plan your week ensuring you do things you enjoy. Tidy your environment. Try a new task or hobby. Go somewhere different. Seek out some laughter (even on the tele) or in good company. Engage in a new hobby or sport. Gardening, yes this actually appeals to some. Golf, tennis, a walk or your favourite hobby, in fact anything you gain pleasure from. My FLOW task this weekend is

_____

DAILY AFFIRMATIONS (Page 37)
I am doing my self-affirmations tomorrow at the following times.
1)_____ 2)_____ 3) _____

"AS IF" (Page 35)
Blow yourself up a bit and believe it, you can hold any state you want. Just colourfully visualise the state you wish for and make it happen in reality. Today I will behave as if...

_____

DON'T OVERTHINK BE HAPPY (Page 90)
Stop overthinking and ruminating trust it will all turn out OK.
I'm thinking optimistically tomorrow about:

_____

GET OFF YOUR BOTTOM (Page 99)
No drug can replace the benefits of exercise. So tomorrow I'm going to:

_____

GRATEFULL THINGS (Page 94)
What are the 3 things I am most grateful for today?

1 _____
2 _____
3 _____

Day   Date   The 5 Minute Focus

Quote...

"Lead with love and light and only good can come out of it"
Will Smith's Grandmother

KINDNESS (Page 96)
I will spread some kindness tomorrow by doing these 5 things; of course you can spread these through the week if you wish.

1 _____
2 _____
3 _____
4 _____
5 _____

SAVOURING (Page 130)
Slow down, live in the moment. Tomorrow I look forward to savouring:

_____

THREE GOOD THINGS (Page 115)
What 3 good things happened today?

1 _____
2 _____
3 _____

PRESS THE ANTI-STRESS BUTTON (Page 50)
When will I take my 3 x 2 minute breaks tomorrow?

1) _____ 2) _____ 3) _____

GET OFF YOUR BOTTOM (Page 99)
No drug can replace the benefits of exercise. So tomorrow I'm going to:

_____

GRATEFULL THINGS (Page 94)
What are the 3 things I am most grateful for today?

1 _____
2 _____
3 _____

Day   Date   (Maybe Sunday?) The 5 Minute Focus

Quote...

"If your judging someone based on who they used to be, obviously its you that's stuck in the past" **Rick Party**

GOALS AND DREAMS (Page 109)
What goals and dreams can I imagine?

_____
_____
_____

WHAT STEPS DO I NEED TO TAKE TO GET THERE (Page 40)
Imagine and picture your 'BEST POSSIBLE SELF'

_____
_____
_____

PRODUCTIVE THINGS (Page 108)
What are the 5 most productive things I can do tomorrow?

1 _____
2 _____
3 _____
4 _____
5 _____

PRESS THE ANTI-STRESS BUTTON (Page 50)
When will I take my 3 x 2 minute breaks tomorrow?

1)_____ 2)_____ 3) _____

GET OFF YOUR BOTTOM (Page 99)
No drug can replace the benefits of exercise. So tomorrow I'm going to:

_____

GRATEFULL THINGS (Page 94)
What are the 3 things I am most grateful for today?

1 _____
2 _____
3 _____

Day   Date   The 5 Minute Focus

Quote...

"If you can meet triumph and disaster, and treat those imposters just the same" (you'll be ok)
Rudyard Kipling

PRODUCTIVE THINGS (Page 108)
What are the 5 most productive things I can do tomorrow?

1 _____
2 _____
3 _____
4 _____
5 _____

DAILY AFFIRMATIONS (Page 37)
I am doing my self-affirmations tomorrow at the following times.

1) _____ 2) _____ 3) _____

SAVOURING (Page 130)
Slow down, live in the moment. Tomorrow I look forward to savouring, these 3 things.

1 _____
2 _____
3 _____

PRESS THE ANTI-STRESS BUTTON (Page 50)
When will I take my 3 x 2 minute breaks tomorrow?

1) _____ 2) _____ 3) _____

GET OFF YOUR BOTTOM (Page 99)
No drug can replace the benefits of exercise. So tomorrow I'm going to:

_____

GRATEFULL THINGS (Page 94)
What are the 3 things I am most grateful for today?

1 _____
2 _____
3 _____

Day   Date   The 5 Minute Focus

Quote...

"Don't dilute yourself, stay at full strength, you are 100% proof" **Martin Hill**

PRODUCTIVE THINGS (Page 108)
What are the 5 most productive things I can do tomorrow?

1 _____
2 _____
3 _____
4 _____
5 _____

DAILY AFFIRMATIONS (Page 37)
I am doing my self-affirmations tomorrow at the following times.

1) _____ 2) _____ 3) _____

KARMA (Page 44)
'What goes around comes around'
My small favour for someone else today is:

PRESS THE ANTI-STRESS BUTTON (Page 50)
When will I take my 3 x 2 minute breaks tomorrow?

1) _____ 2) _____ 3) _____

GET OFF YOUR BOTTOM (Page 99)
No drug can replace the benefits of exercise. So tomorrow I'm going to:

GRATEFULL THINGS (Page 94)
What are the 3 things I am most grateful for today?

1 _____
2 _____
3 _____

Day _____ Date _____ The 5 Minute Focus

Quote...

"Two wrongs don't make a right."
Margaret Ashman (my mum)

PRODUCTIVE THINGS (Page 108)
What are the 5 most productive things I can do tomorrow?

1 _____
2 _____
3 _____
4 _____
5 _____

DAILY AFFIRMATIONS (Page 37)
I am doing my self-affirmations tomorrow at the following times.

1) _____ 2) _____ 3) _____

'SMILE' (Page 125)
Smile at yourself in the mirror, and be proud, you've done your best!
I'm smiling at my self tomorrow 3 times at the following times:

1) _____ 2) _____ 3) _____

PRESS THE ANTI-STRESS BUTTON (Page 50)
When will I take my 3 x 2 minute breaks tomorrow?

1) _____ 2) _____ 3) _____

GET OFF YOUR BOTTOM (Page 99)
No drug can replace the benefits of exercise. So tomorrow I'm going to:

_____

GRATEFULL THINGS (Page 94)
What are the 3 things I am most grateful for today?

1 _____
2 _____
3 _____

Day   Date   The 5 Minute Focus

Quote...

***"This isn't getting the baby a new dress"* Peter Hill (My dad, meaning get some work done!)**

PRODUCTIVE THINGS (Page 108)
What are the 5 most productive things I can do tomorrow?

1 _____
2 _____
3 _____
4 _____
5 _____

DAILY AFFIRMATIONS (Page 37)
I am doing my self-affirmations tomorrow at the following times.

1)_____ 2)_____ 3) _____

HAPPINESS 'REFRAME' (Page 86)
If anything pops into my head to annoy me I will simply deal with it, let it go, or think about it from a new perspective. My new perspective tomorrow is:

_____

PRESS THE ANTI-STRESS BUTTON (Page 50)
When will I take my 3 x 2 minute breaks tomorrow?

1)_____ 2)_____ 3) _____

GET OFF YOUR BOTTOM (Page 99)
No drug can replace the benefits of exercise. So tomorrow I'm going to:

_____

GRATEFULL THINGS (Page 94)
What are the 3 things I am most grateful for today?

1 _____
2 _____
3 _____

Day   Date   The 5 Minute Focus

Quote...

"You need to BELIEVE to ACHIEVE, if you don't it wont happen" **Nigel Adkins**

GET IN THE FLOW THIS WEEKEND (Page 127)

Try your own ideas, were all so different (or a few of the following) Listen to music. Visit a really good friend. Read a book. Cook something new. Get a cuddle. Plan your dreams. Plan your week ensuring you do things you enjoy. Tidy your environment. Try a new task or hobby. Go somewhere different. Seek out some laughter (even on the tele) or in good company. Engage in a new hobby or sport. Gardening, yes this actually appeals to some. Golf, tennis, a walk or your favourite hobby, in fact anything you gain pleasure from. My FLOW task this weekend is

_____

DAILY AFFIRMATIONS (Page 37)
I am doing my self-affirmations tomorrow at the following times.
1)_____ 2)_____ 3) _____

"AS IF" (Page 35)
Blow yourself up a bit and believe it, you can hold any state you want. Just colourfully visualise the state you wish for and make it happen in reality. Today I will behave as if...

_____

DON'T OVERTHINK BE HAPPY (Page 90)
Stop overthinking and ruminating trust it will all turn out OK.
I'm thinking optimistically tomorrow about:

_____

GET OFF YOUR BOTTOM (Page 99)
No drug can replace the benefits of exercise. So tomorrow I'm going to:

_____

GRATEFULL THINGS (Page 94)
What are the 3 things I am most grateful for today?

1 _____
2 _____
3 _____

Day   Date   The 5 Minute Focus

Quote...

ALL IN... 'EVERY TIME'
Be confident and just be your very best self. Martin Hill

KINDNESS (Page 96)
I will spread some kindness tomorrow by doing these 5 things; of course you can spread these through the week if you wish.

1 _____
2 _____
3 _____
4 _____
5 _____

SAVOURING (Page 130)
Slow down, live in the moment. Tomorrow I look forward to savouring:

_____

THREE GOOD THINGS (Page 115)
What 3 good things happened today?

1 _____
2 _____
3 _____

PRESS THE ANTI-STRESS BUTTON (Page 50)
When will I take my 3 x 2 minute breaks tomorrow?

1) _____   2) _____   3) _____

GET OFF YOUR BOTTOM (Page 99)
No drug can replace the benefits of exercise. So tomorrow I'm going to:

_____

GRATEFULL THINGS (Page 94)
What are the 3 things I am most grateful for today?

1 _____
2 _____
3 _____

Well done, you've just completed

The Happiness Scheme.

I hope this book has made a positive influence on your life, if it has please take a little time out to let me know by emailing the following address,

martinhill@thehappinesssheme.com

You could even classify this as a kindness task! ☺☺

Further recommended inspirational reading:

Staying Sane – Dr Raj Persaud, an eminent psychiatrist and broadcaster cuts through myths and taboos offering strategies and advice to maintain a balanced life.

Reasons to Stay Alive – Matt Haig writes about his real life experiences in dealing with depression in a book which is moving, funny and heart lifting.

The How of Happiness – Sonja Lyubomirsky Professor of Psychology at the University of California details the wealth of her scientific research in a guide to finding real happiness.

Mindfulness – Professor Mark Williams and Dr Danny Penman team up to offer a practical guide to finding peace through mindful based cognitive therapy (MBCT) and mediation.

Awakening the Brain – Charlotte A Tomaino PhD is a clinical neuropsychologist. Her book discusses ways of awakening your brain and expanding your consciousness.

The Official Guide to Success – Tom Hopkins discusses ways to achieve your goals and gain success.

Notes and references

1) Neck, C. P. and Manz, C. C. (1992), Thought self-leadership: The influence of self-talk and mental imagery on performance. J. Organiz. Behav., 13: 681–699. doi:10.1002/job.4030130705

(2) Briñol, P., Gascoó, M., Petter, R.E., & Horcajo, J. (2012). Treating Thoughts as Material Objects Can Increase or Decrease Their Impact on Evaluation. Psychological Science.

(3) Brummett BH, et al. Prediction of all-cause mortality by the Minnesota Multiphasic Personality Inventory Optimism-Pessimism Scale scores: Study of a college sample during a 40-year follow-up period. Mayo Clinic Proceedings. 2006;81:1541.

(4) Lindsay EK, Creswell JD. Helping the self help others: self-affirmation increases self-compassion and pro-social behaviors. Frontiers in Psychology. 2014;5:421. doi:10.3489/fpsyg.2014.00421.

(5) Menahem S, et al. Forgiveness in psychotherapy: The key to healing. The Journal of Clinical Psychology: In Session. 2013;69:829.

(6) Brown, Kirk Warren; Ryan, Richard M. Journal of Personality and Social Psychology The benefits of being present: Mindfulness and its role in psychological well-being. , Vol 84(4), Apr 2003, 822-848.

(7) science.house.gov/sites/republicans.science.house.gov/files/documents/hearings/032107_gore.pdf

(8) Michl LC, McLaughlin KA, Shepherd K, Nolen-Hoeksema S. Rumination as a Mechanism Linking Stressful Life Events to Symptoms of Depression and Anxiety: Longitudinal Evidence in Early Adolescents and Adults. Journal of abnormal psychology. 2013;122(2):349-352. doi:10.1037/a0031994.

(9) Sansone RA, Sansone LA. Gratitude and Well Being: The Benefits of Appreciation. Psychiatry (Edgmont). 2010;7(11):18-22.

(10) Otake K, Shimai S, Tanaka-Matsumi J, Otsui K, Fredrickson Bl. Happy People Become Happier Through Kindness: A Counting Kindnesses Intervention. Journal of happiness studies. 2006;7(3):361- 375. doi:10.1007/s10902-005-3650-z.

(11) Kraft TL, Pressman SD, (2012) Psychological Science. Grin and bear it: The influence of manipulated facial expression on the stress response.

(12) http://greatergood.berkeley.edu/article/item/10_steps_to_savoring_the_good_things_in_life

13)(https://science.house.gov/sites/republicans.science.house.gov/files/documents/hearings/032107_gore.pdf_Al Gore
(14) Tales of a Traveler (1824), Preface, p. 7. (20) Hershberger (15) PJ. Prescribing happiness: Positive psychology and family medicine. Family Medicine. 2005;37:630.
(15)http://sonjalyubomirsky.com/wpcontent/themes/sonjalyubomirsky/papers/LSS2005.pdf
(16) J. C. Coulson, J. McKenna, M. Field Exercising at work and self-reported work performance; International Journal of Workplace Health Management
(17) Alice M. Isen and Barbara Means (1983). The Influence of Positive Affect on Decision-Making Strategy
(18) The Framingham Heart Study BMJ 2008;337:a2338
(20) Sharma A, Madaan V, Petty FD. Exercise for Mental Health. Primary Care Companion to The Journal of Clinical Psychiatry. 2006;8(2):106.

Martin Hill is available for presentations and meetings to discuss his ideas further. He warmly welcomes presentations to schools, colleges and universities. He is also available for one-to-one confidential meetings with business directors and professionals. For further information please don't hesitate to email the following address.

martinhill@thehappinesssheme.com